The Caves of Northumberland

© Chris Scaife, 2019

All Rights Reserved. No part of this publication may be reproduced, stored in a retrieval system, or transmitted in any form or by any means – electronic, mechanical, photocopying, recording, or otherwise – without prior written permission from the publisher or a licence permitting restricted copying issued by the Copyright Licensing Agency, 90 Tottenham Court Road, London W1P 0LA. This book may not be lent, resold, hired out or otherwise disposed of by trade in any form of binding or cover other than that in which it is published, without the prior consent of the publisher.

Moral Rights: The author has asserted his moral right to be identified as the Author of this Work.

Published by Sigma Leisure – an imprint of
Sigma Press, Stobart House, Pontyclerc, Penybanc Road, Ammanford, Carmarthenshire SA18 3HP.

British Library Cataloguing in Publication Data
A CIP record for this book is available from the British Library.

ISBN: 978-1-910758-43-4

Typesetting and Design by: Sigma Press, Ammanford.

Cover: Main photograph: Looking out from Brotherston's Hole Cave 10 © Chris Scaife; Top photographs (left to right): Carolina Smith de la Fuente in the entrance to Burgess' Cove 1, Berwick © Chris Scaife; Chris Scaife in Seagull's Welly Resurgence © Ben Coult; Niyati Gupta, Layla Taleb and Carolina Smith de la Fuente in Cateran Hole © Chris Scaife; Chris Scaife in Holly Tree Hole, High Cove © Don Miller.

Photographs: © Chris Scaife, unless otherwise stated

Maps: © Chris Scaife

Printed by: Akcent Media Ltd

Disclaimer: the information in this book is given in good faith and is believed to be correct at the time of publication. Caving is a potentially dangerous activity and all participants do so at their own risk. No responsibility is accepted by either the author or publisher for errors or omissions, or for any loss or injury however caused. Only you can judge your own fitness, competence and experience.

The Caves of Northumberland

Chris Scaife

Foreword

Northumberland is not England's best-known cave-bearing county. It's up there at the top of England, a bit beyond the areas with lots of blue (limestone) on the geological maps. It just catches a smidgeon of the Pennines in Allendale and South Tynedale, but north of the Tyne spreads endless broad acres of gritstone moorlands, with the odd thin limestone band. So most of its caves are caves for connoisseurs, and Chris Scaife is a connoisseur, and to be honest they are the ones I enjoy reading about. Every one a collector's piece, set in an unparalleled landscape rich in stories; who could ask for more? And the caves, the geology, the landscape and the stories all go together: I think that is what comes across in these pages. An 8m long gritstone cave and Penyghent Pot, they share in being dark and underground, but that is about it. The 8m long gritstone cave certainly hurts less, but is small enough to take your time over and savour; set in its context it is a delight. And setting-in-context is what Chris does really well here; he has provided a book not only to act as a guide in the great outdoors, but also one that is a guidebook to one's own inner grotto, the caver's personal inside world, which will trigger memories and imagination when dreaming before the winter fire, something I increasingly find myself doing these days. 'Make a day of it' he often says, and gives us a recipe for the making of many excellent days, days that will result in a richer acquaintanceship with a whole host of good localities and good things.

I have been privileged to be involved in the exploration and surveying of some of these caves, most of it quite some time ago. This included a few trips down the biggest-Northumberland-cave-of-all, Ayleburn Mine Cave, currently sadly inaccessible – maybe these pages will inspire some speleohound to find a new way into it; that may not be too difficult. I have also sampled a selection of the intriguing gritstone caves and cavelets further north, including places like Cateran Hole, yes a slip rift, but what slipped where? These are places that stay with you. And Northumberland is not an area that has been 'worked out'; hopefully this book will only be the first edition, with a revised, improved and expanded version ready to leap onto our shelves in a year or two's time. So enjoy this one, and await the next…

Pete Ryder (Moldwarps Speleo Group)
March 2019

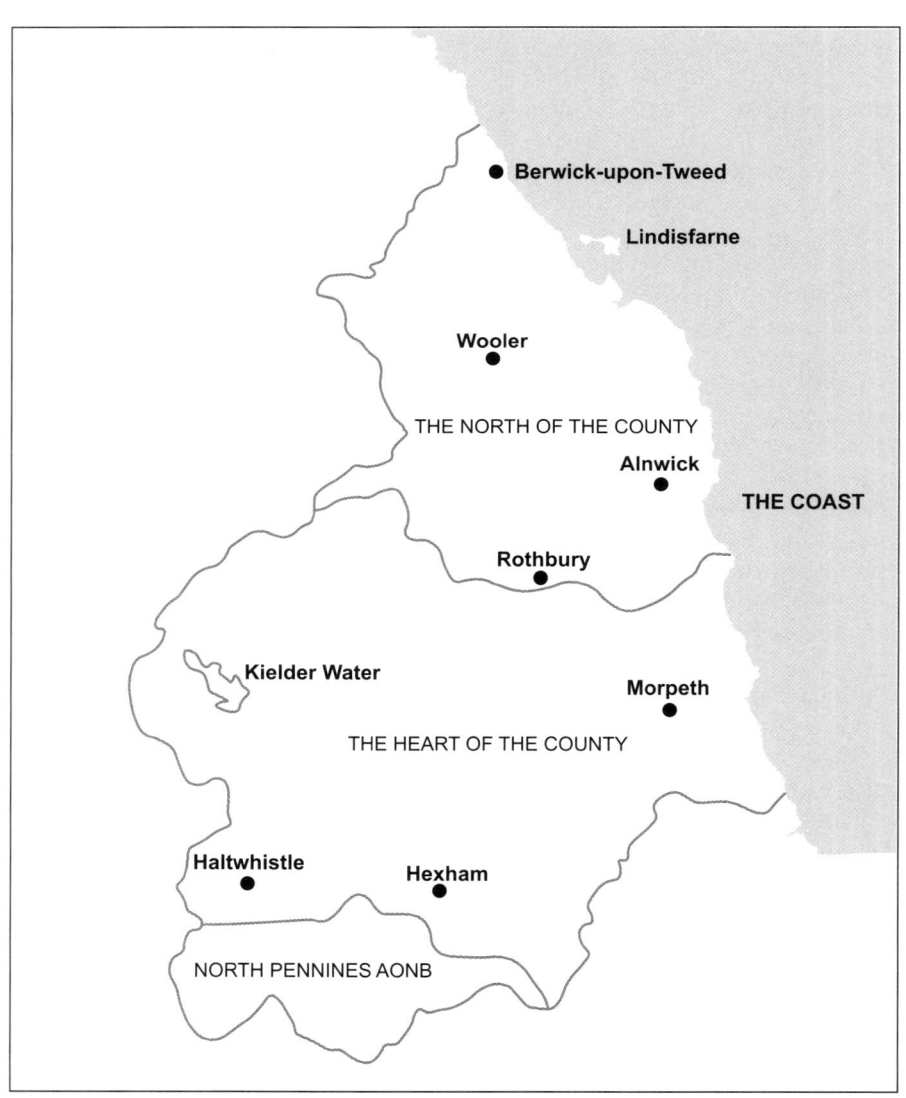

Map of Northumberland showing the main guidebook areas

Contents

Foreword	5
Introduction	9
Acknowledgements	14
The North of the County	**15**
Roughting Linn Cave	19
St Cuthbert's Cave	22
Cateran Hole	25
Cateran Rift	28
Doubting Victoria Cave	31
Thomas Wedderburn's Hole	33
Coe Crag Cave	36
Pupienus Hole	38
Nine Year Aud Hole	40
The Heart of the County	**43**
Huel Crag Rifts	46
South Yardhope Caves	49
High Cove	52
Key Heugh Caves	56
Ward's Hill Quarry Caves	59
Wire Hole	62
The Wanney Byer	65
Shaftoe Hall	69
Hartburn Grotto	72

Alloa Lea Quarry Cave	75
Bellcrag Cave	78
Queen's Cave	81
North Pennines Area of Outstanding Natural Beauty	**84**
Simsholm Well	87
Ayleburn Mine Cave	90
Ayleburn Caves 1 and 2	94
Ayleburn Pot	97
Hartleycleugh Quarry Cave	100
Seagull's Welly Pot and Resurgence	103
Tutu's Welly Pot	106
Elpha Green Caves	110
The Coast	**114**
Berwick-upon-Tweed Sea Caves	118
Lindisfarne Caves	133
Rumbling Kern Caves	137
Crag Point Caves	140
Cullercoats Caves	144
Minor caves	149
Glossary of caving terms	151
History of caving guidebooks that have included this region	152
Index	154
About the author	155

Introduction

As with many cavers, my first experiences of caving were in the potholes of the Yorkshire Dales. Although walking, cycling and climbing had allowed me to get to know Northumberland fairly well, caving was always something to do elsewhere. Indeed, I had made countless journeys to the major caving regions in the UK, including Yorkshire, South Wales, the Peak District and the Mendip Hills, before ever venturing underground in Northumberland.

The first caves I visited in this county were Roughting Linn Cave and Cateran Hole, far to the north. I was immediately struck by the unusual nature of these caves: the former an extremely rare elliptic tube in sandstone beside a stunning waterfall; the latter a remarkable walking passage appearing unexpectedly in heather moorland, entered via mysterious stone steps from a bygone era. I realised from the beginning that the caves of Northumberland were special and worth investigating further.

I soon learnt that there were fascinating tales attached to some of these holes and, delving deeper, it became apparent that there were many caves that had not been recorded in any detail. Accordingly, I have pored over old caving club journals, maps and Victorian guidebooks, wandered hillsides and rocky shores, to come up with this first comprehensive guide to Northumberland's caves.

I hope that this book will appeal to all those with an interest in the outdoors and in Northumberland, whether as a resident or visitor. I hope that cavers will see, as I have seen, that many excellent days out are to be had in this wonderful county; and that those who have not been caving before will be drawn to take their first steps into the underworld.

Safety

Before venturing out, be prepared for changes in the weather and pack appropriately. Always tell someone where you are going and when you expect to be back, and leave that person with enough information that they could call the rescue services in the event that you are long overdue.

In the event of a coastal emergency, dial 999 or 112 and ask to speak to the Coastguard. In the event of an emergency inland, call 999 or 112 and ask to speak to the Police, then request Mountain Rescue and explain the situation thoroughly. The information that the rescue team would want includes: number of people involved, their names and ages; any information about injuries sustained; any potential hazards to the rescue team; location of the party and information on the best access to the location. The Mountain Rescue team will decide whether it is necessary to involve a Cave Rescue team. Bear in mind, however, that the nearest designated Cave Rescue teams are many, many miles away in the Yorkshire Dales.

Caving is a potentially dangerous activity and all participants do so at their own risk. The author accepts no liability for any injury howsoever caused.

Access

The vast majority of the caves in this guidebook are on open access land, where there are unlikely to be any objections to the presence of visitors. However, a small number – such as the caves at Ayleburn, Elpha Green and Hartleycleugh – are on private land and it is the responsibility of all cavers to seek permission from the landowners prior to any visit. Inclusion of a cave in this guidebook does not mean that access is allowed or will be granted. Whilst every effort has been made to identify the landowner within each entry for which permission is currently needed, land ownership may change over time. If in doubt, the best advice is normally to call in at the nearest farmhouse and ask politely.

Walking around the Northumberland countryside in full caving gear may arouse more curiosity and suspicion than it would in the more established caving regions, such as the Yorkshire Dales and South Wales. Most caves in this book do not require full caving gear, but for those that do, it may be preferable to carry the kit to the entrance in a rucksack.

For more information on access arrangements for cavers in the north of England, please consult the website of the Council of Northern Caving Clubs (CNCC): **https://cncc.org.uk/**

Not everyone out there likes intrepid souls and from time to time entrances to wonderful caves are sealed by tepid souls, who no doubt believe that they are making the world a safer place but care naught for adventure. If you find a cave entrance unexpectedly sealed, or find that access arrangements have changed since the publication of this guide, please contact the CNCC to let them know.

Difficulty Grading

UK caves are traditionally graded from 1 to 5, with Grade 1 being the easiest. In Northumberland, the majority of the caves are Grades 1 and 2, with just Hartleycleugh Quarry Cave and Ayleburn Mine Cave Grade 3. For the purposes of this guide, which is aimed as much at beginners as it is at experienced cavers, I think it more appropriate to use this alternative grading system:

Easy – Caves that are accessible to most reasonably fit individuals, including novices. Caving equipment will usually not be required, except for a light, although clothes are unlikely to remain completely clean.

Moderate – Caves that require some element of caving skill, and caving equipment, but without any particularly serious difficulties. A caving oversuit and wellies, as well as a helmet and light, are strongly recommended.

Difficult – For experienced cavers only.

The best way to gain caving experience is to join a caving club. This excellent website has information on caving clubs suitable for novices: https://newtocaving.com/

Maps
At the beginning of each cave's entry I have identified the relevant Ordnance Survey 1:25,000 map, by map number and title. I have used eight-figure grid references for cave entrances and several other important features that are not easy to find using the map alone. In general, for obvious features that will normally be found using the map, such as parking spots, I have used six-figure grid references.

Wildlife
Northumberland is a sparsely populated county with great geographical diversity, and consequently there is a wide variety of wildlife to be seen. During visits to the caves in this book I have encountered, amongst other things: stoat, weasel, roe deer, grey seal, red squirrel, goshawk, common scoter, pied flycatcher, peregrine falcon, woodcock, cuckoo, viviparous lizard and adder.

Some of the caves in this guide are situated at crags that are important nesting sites for protected birds. The most vulnerable time for nesting birds is generally between late February and early June, when it is advised that visits to Key Heugh and Doubting Victoria Cave are avoided. At any site, if it appears that any wildlife is uncomfortable with your presence during breeding season, please leave the caves for another day.

Within the caves themselves, invertebrates such as moths and the completely harmless European cave spider, *Meta menardi*, are likely to be seen. Fish such as brown trout are occasionally seen in underground streamways and may be etiolated, or blanched, if they have been in darkness for a long time. Bats are infrequently encountered in Northumberland's caves, but if you are lucky enough to see them, please remember that all UK bats are protected species and are not to be disturbed. They typically hibernate from November to March, but may also roost in caves in daylight hours during the summer. Many sea caves contain rock pools and are therefore good places to see small fish, crabs, sea anemones and starfish.

Nomenclature

Many of the caves in Northumberland have been known locally for centuries and consequently have names whose origins are lost in the mists of time. More recent subterranean discoveries have been named, as is traditional in the caving world, by their original explorers. Where the information is available, I have used the known names for all caves in this book. At certain sites, especially sea cliffs, there are sometimes numerous caves very close together and very little information in print or online about any existing names, so I have had to name them myself. No doubt some of these will have been given names at some point so I apologise to anyone who has previously named a cave in Northumberland and is now missing out on the joy of seeing that name in print.

Format for cave descriptions

Each cave, or group of caves, is given its own entry within the appropriate geographical section. Where caves are very close together, of a similar nature and have intertwined histories I have described them together. There are some caves that are close together and will normally be visited in conjunction with others (e.g. Cateran Hole, Cateran Rift and Doubting Victoria Cave; Seagull's Welly Pot and Tutu's Welly Pot) but have been given individual entries because they are of a different nature and the stories of their original exploration are distinct.

The entries are set out thusly:

- Name of the cave
- Length in metres
- Depth in metres, if applicable
- Rock type
- Ordnance Survey 1:25,000 map on which the entrance is located
- Eight figure grid reference
- Difficulty grading

- **Introduction**
  Some information about the history of the cave and its environs.

- **The route**
  A detailed description of how to get to the cave from a suitable parking place, followed by a description of the cave itself. Whilst I have described the route from a parking place, I certainly do not wish to imply that driving is the only way to get around; indeed, many of the caves in this book are suitable for visits by other modes of transport, particularly cycling.

- **Make a day of it**
  Ideas for other activities that may be of interest once back in the sublunary world.

Acknowledgements

I am forever in debt to all my chthonic companions, past and present, who have helped nurture my love of the tenebrous parts of the world.

A special mention is owed to the following: Don Miller joined me on many of the trips to Northumberland's nether reaches and his enthusiasm helped get this project off, or under, the ground. Peter Ryder, as well as writing the foreword and finding quite a few of the caves in Northumberland, has been an invaluable source of information on all things speleological, archaeological and historical. I have bombarded John Cordingley, Sam Allshorn and Peter Eagan with questions and they have all been very helpful. Ben Coult has helped a great deal, both by sharing his knowledge of the North Pennines and by joining me on a number of caving trips in the area.

I could probably not have written this book without Carolina Smith de la Fuente, who has not only joined me on numerous excursions to these caves but also shared an office with me while I wrote this book. Many of her own working days have been interrupted while I have read aloud every single paragraph. Sorry.

THE NORTH OF THE COUNTY

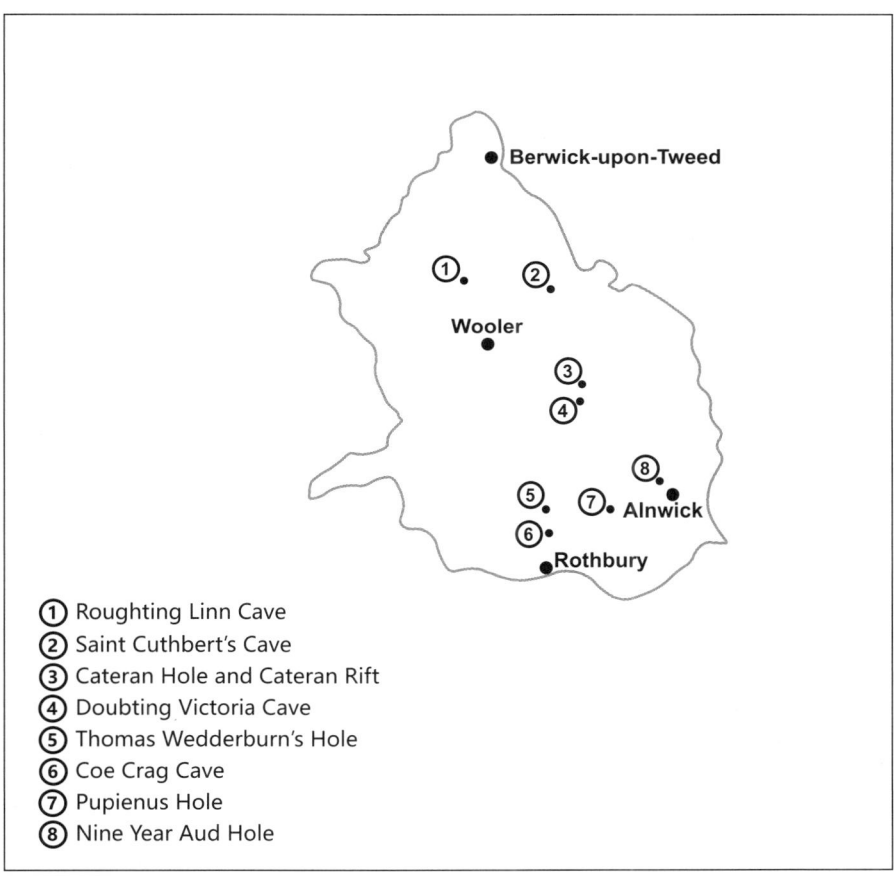

Cave locations in the North of the County

Much of the northernmost part of Northumberland is a wild and remote area, dominated in the west by the rounded, rolling Cheviot Hills, forming part of the border with Scotland. Also known as The White Lands owing to their

Prehistoric rock art near Roughting Linn Cave

extensive grasslands, the Cheviots are formed principally of igneous andesite and granite. The Cheviot itself, at 815m, is the highest point in Northumberland and there are several other peaks nearby that surpass the height of 2,000 feet (610m) and thus qualify as English Mountains. To the east is less mountainous, but visitors will still find solitude, beauty and intrigue here.

The history of this area is very rich indeed. Some of Britain's finest prehistoric rock art is found at Roughting Linn, and there are other cup and ring marked rocks at various sites. There are stone circles in several locations, such as near Duddo, Threestoneburn and Doddington. Iron Age Hillforts are found in a few places, with the best example at Yeavering Bell. Saint Cuthbert, patron saint of Northumbria, is inextricably linked to the history of north Northumberland and the long-distance walk St Cuthbert's Way, a 100km (62 miles) trail from Melrose in Scotland to Holy Island, passes by St Cuthbert's Cave, said to be where Saint Cuthbert's body was taken by monks fleeing Viking raids on Lindisfarne in the year 875.

For centuries this Border region was involved in on-off warfare between England and Scotland, beginning with William the Conqueror's Harrying of the North, and the Scottish King Malcolm III's subsequent border raids, and not coming to an end until well after the Union of England and Scotland Act, which followed the coronation of King James I of England and Ireland, or VI of Scotland, in 1603. With continual conflict and invasions, the practice of reiving became the norm. The Border reivers would raid their neighbouring farms and villages, often taking hostages as well as food and riches. In response to this chaotic state, March Law, or Border Law, was introduced, with Wardens of the Marches established to administer the laws.

The caves in this section are all formed in sandstone, little affected by weather conditions and most do not require any special equipment. You don't even need a light for some of these. History and folklore abound, and fascinating local legends are associated with many of these caves.

There are historical records of a small cave, known as Cartington Cove, just below Old Rothbury Hillfort, at NU 044 019. This site contained cup and ring marked rocks, on the walls of the cave, and according to local tradition was linked by an underground passage to Cartington Castle, which is about 3 miles (5km) to the north. Unfortunately, this cave and its artwork were destroyed by quarrying sometime after 1859.

A legendary cave, known as the Laidley Worm's Cave, is described in the ballad of The Laidly Worm of Spindlestone Heugh. A kind Northumbrian king, on the throne at Bamburgh Castle, married a witch after the death of his first wife. The king's son, Childe Wynd, had travelled to distant lands, but his daughter, Margaret, remained at Bamburgh. The witch turned Princess Margaret into a dragon, the Laidly Worm, which used a cave and trough at Spindlestone on the Great Whin Sill. Childe Wynd returned and saved the day by repeatedly kissing the dragon to return her to human form, before turning the witch into a toad. Whilst Laidley Worm's Trough is still marked on Ordnance Survey maps at NZ 156 339, the stone trough described in the past has gone – although there is a pond at this site – and the cave was destroyed by quarrying in the 19th century.

An article published in the *Newcastle Journal* on the 20th of August 1842 described a very extensive cave system on Alnwick Moor, in the limestone to the south-west of the race ground, about a furlong (roughly 200m) from the hamlet of Hobberlaw. The article stated that two openings had been found by removing some rocks, revealing a cavern 'of considerable extent'. The passages are described as 'neatly arched, approaching to the order and regularity of a work of art'. There had at one time been plentiful formations in the cave, but many of these were stolen by the numerous visitors.

There is a tale that the Duke of Northumberland was once hunting in this locale, when two of his hounds pursued a fox into the cave and were lost for days. One of the men explored the cave so far that he was able to hear footsteps above his head, coming from Hobberlaw, a furlong as the crow flies from the entrance. The emaciated, famished dogs were eventually rescued, one on the 15th day, and one on the 16th day.

The area in which this cave entrance is thought to have been located is now a very overgrown disused quarry with brambles and nettles and no sign of an entrance can be found at present. For now, this must be considered a lost cave, but perhaps one day it will be re-discovered, along with Reynard, whose fate has never been determined.

Roughting Linn Cave

10m
Fell Sandstone
Map: 339 – Kelso, Coldstream and Lower Tweed Valley
NT 9823 3679
Easy

Introduction
This is a glorious place. Within a few minutes of leaving your car, you can see a fantastic waterfall, one of the UK's finest prehistoric rock art sites and a highly unusual cave.

Roughting Linn Cave, named after the nearby bellowing waterfall on the Broomridgedean Burn, was first recorded by Graham Mullan of the University of Bristol Spelaeological Society, and his dogs, in 1985. It appears to be a phreatic tube, which would make it extremely rare, as this method of cave formation, or speleogenesis, is almost exclusively found in limestone caves. Phreatic action forms cave passages entirely under water, as opposed to vadose action, which is when a stream flowing through a passage erodes the floor.

The route
The parking spot is found by turning off the A697 at the Maelmin Heritage Trail, just south of Milfield, and following this road for 5.8km (3.6 miles). Park at NT 984 366, beside the minor road leading south from the junction opposite Routin Linn Farm, and follow the bridleway north-west, signposted 'Public Bridleway Goats Crag ¾'. After 120m, there are small paths on both sides of the bridleway. Take the path on the left, which goes downhill and follows the stream up to the majestic, photogenic waterfall. The tubular cave entrance is on the right after 160m.

Roughting Linn Cave is an elliptic tube, with some scalloping visible, indicating the flow of water in its formation. The cave is a crawl, lowering to flat-out, then after 5m there is an easy squeeze into a small final chamber. If nobody has visited for a while, the decaying leaves on the floor can almost fill the passage and make the squeeze towards the end feel like an autumnal

Chris Scaife at the squeeze *Photo by Don Miller*

free-dive, so it may be prudent to remove some on the way. Just above and to the right of the cave entrance, there is a small second cave, a 3m tube.

Make a day of it

The carved outcrop of rock a short distance to the east of Roughting Linn is adorned with ancient carvings and is notable for its size, as well as the variety of the cup and ring marks. To see this extraordinary sight, return along the small path and continue across the bridleway, undulating through the earthworks for 100m. The path then forks; take the left fork and after 20m you will reach the prehistoric petroglyphs, at NT 9839 3674. The path south from this magnificent outcrop reaches the road after 30m, and the parking spot is just 60m down this road.

By following the bridleway that passes Routin Linn Farm, Goatscrag Hill will soon be reached on the right-hand side. It is worth exploring this crag, which has a rock shelter believed to have been used in Mesolithic times, and in which a Bronze Age burial has been discovered. The views from the top are impressive, with the Cheviot Hills to the west and the North Sea to the east. Return to the bridleway and continue heading west, and after about 800m you will reach Ford Moss Colliery and Nature Reserve. This interesting place can be explored by a 3km circular walk.

Maelmin Heritage Trail is just outside the village of Milfield and it is worth a stop here en route to see the reproduced wooden henge, Stone Age hut and Dark Ages house, all visited by a short walking trail.

To get to Flodden Battlefield, follow the A697 north from Milfield for 5.7km (3.5 miles) and then turn left towards Branxton. Follow this narrow road to Branxton, then turn left at the far end of the village to get to the car park. There is an excellent walk around the battlefield, with interpretation boards. It was in this battle that James IV of Scotland became the last British king to die in combat.

St Cuthbert's Cave

7m
Fell Sandstone
Map: 340 – Holy Island and Bamburgh
NU 0591 3525
Easy

Introduction
Also known as Cuddy's Cave, this is one of the best known caves in Northumberland, thanks to its associations with the ascetic Saint Cuthbert of the early Northumbrian church.

There are several suggestions as to how the cave got its name, but the most popular local tale is that this is where the saint's body was taken by Eardulf, Bishop of Lindisfarne, and abbot Eadred, following a Viking attack on Lindisfarne in the year 875. Eardulf and Eadred wandered for seven years before the remains were laid to rest in St Cuthbert's Church in Chester-le-Street. Since 1104 Saint Cuthbert's remains have been housed in Durham Cathedral. In that year, when Cuthbert's coffin was opened, a small leather-bound book, the Gospel of St John, was found inside. Now known as St Cuthbert Gospel and housed in the British Library, this is the oldest surviving example of Western bookbinding.

Evidence of the local importance of this cave is demonstrated by the fact that the name of the car park is St Cuthbert's Cave Car Park and the wood in which the cave is found is called St Cuthbert's Cave Wood.

In early Victorian times the cave was used as a lambing shed, with a stone wall enclosing the entrance. Later the cave was consecrated and used as a burial site for the Leather family, who owned the cave for much of the 20th century. Since 1981 the cave and the wood have been managed by the National Trust.

The route
There are few caves in the UK for which route finding is as straightforward as it is for St Cuthbert's Cave. The cave is signposted from the St Cuthbert's Cave National Trust Car Park at Holburn Grange (NU 051 351) and is found by following a clearly marked path.

Don Miller in St Cuthbert's Cave

Upon leaving the car park, turn left and follow the track up the hill for about 600m. At the top of this track there is a gate, and a stile, then take the track to the right through the gorse. Follow this grassy track for about 500m, keeping to the right where the track splits, to a gate at the corner of the wood. A very short distance after passing through this gate, turn left up the path towards the large rock outcrop, with the very obvious cave.

This large rock shelter is 3m high and 24m across. The back wall is 7m back from the cliff face and a natural rock pillar is present in the middle of the cave. There is no need to bring a light for this one, unless of course you choose to visit at night-time or during a total eclipse of the sun. There are also several very small caves and rock shelters, none exceeding 3m in length, on the south-western slope of nearby Greensheen Hill (NU 056 358).

Make a day of it
A pleasant circuit can now be followed by heading back to the gate at the corner of the wood, turning right and walking uphill alongside the wood. Follow St Cuthbert's Way in a north-easterly direction for about 1km, to where

it joins both St Oswald's Way and the Northumberland Coast Path at NU 067 359. Turn left and follow the stone track to the woodland, then follow the sign to Holburn. This path will take you past Holburn Lake and Moss nature reserve and Raven's Crag. The path soon starts heading south again, to a T-junction at NU 046 361. Right here leads to the small village of Holburn and left leads back towards the start.

From NU 067 359, St Oswald's Way and the Northumberland Coast Path, which share ground here, can be followed to the south-east for about 5km to the pleasant village of Belford.

Cateran Hole

35m
Fell Sandstone
Map: 332 – Alnwick and Amble (although the parking place is on map 340 – Holy Island and Bamburgh)
NU 1023 2367
Easy

Introduction

The remote Chillingham Hills offer dramatic views, fascinating historical sites and, most importantly of all, several very interesting caves. The most interesting of these is undoubtedly the family-friendly easy walking passage known as Cateran Hole. This cave is liable to surprise the first-time visitor, as the heathery moorland of the gentle northern slopes of Cateran Hill, devoid of crags or escarpments, seems an unlikely place to find such a feature.

This is a cave that is steeped in history and legend. Traditionally believed to have been part of a great tunnel leading to Hen Hole on the Cheviot, more than 17km away, there is obvious evidence of human activity in this cave, with its carved steps at the entrance, and a 12m long shelf lining one wall just inside the entrance. Many believe that these modifications were made by the Border reivers. Cateran Hill, on which this cave is found, has a strong link with the Border reivers, gangs of warriors, freebooters or raiders – also known as caterans – who worked along the Anglo-Scottish border from the 13th to the 17th century.

This cave is the county's best example of a mass-movement cave in sandstone, formed by vertical fractures in the rock. Elsewhere on Cateran Hill there are several other examples of similar activity, which has resulted in open gorges, or trenches, rather than caves. The surrounding area is wonderfully remote and includes many prehistoric delights.

The route

Park beside the North Charlton to Hepburn road, west of Quarry House, at NU 101 246. Take the path signposted 'Public Bridleway Blawearie 2 Old Bewick 3½' for 800m and take the first left, which is signposted 'Public

Bridleway', heading to Cateran Hill. About 500m along this bridleway, just after the path starts to get steeper (NU 1008 2364) there is a small rock in the middle of the path, with the carved letters, 'CH' and an arrow pointing to a path on the left. Follow this faint path diagonally left and after 150m you will reach a small grassy depression in the heather moorland, with carved stone steps leading down into the cave entrance. If unable to find the small path, the cave can be found by walking towards the top of the hill, then walking back towards Quarry House in such a line that the tall radio aerial behind the house appears just inside the edge of the wood beside the farm.

Descend the six stone steps into this fascinating cave. The entrance is 3m high and 75cm wide and the cave begins as a walking passage with impressively straight walls, widening after 14m. At 25m from the entrance, the pebbled floor gives way to soft ground. The walking passage continues until a short, sandy crawl is needed to reach the final chamber, which is 2m high and 1m wide. The crawl at the end is often completely dry, but occasionally sumps in wet weather.

Chris Scaife in Cateran Hole   *Photo by Don Miller*

Make a day of it

Cateran Hole can easily be combined with visits to Cateran Rift and Doubting Victoria Cave. There is splendid countryside around here and visitors are encouraged to walk or cycle in the surrounding area. The road running between North Charlton in the east and Hepburn in the west is one of the finest roads in Northumberland on a bike, and keen cyclists should find plenty of options if wishing to incorporate this into a longer circuit.

Some very interesting archaeological sites can be found by returning to the large bridleway heading south from the suggested parking spot. This can be followed to the idyllically situated abandoned cottage at Blawearie, close to which is the restored Bronze Age Blawearie Cairn (NU 0816 2231). South-west of here, at NU 075 216, is the Iron Age Old Bewick Hillfort, a place with fantastic views, as well as a Second World War pillbox. Following the fence down to the east from the hillfort, look out for two prominent flat boulders, one on either side of the fence, as these both have fine cup and ring marks.

Close to the road, about 3km north of Blawearie is Ros Hill, also known as Ros Castle, at NU 081 253. This is the site of a 3,000-year-old Iron Age hillfort and a marvellous viewpoint, as it is the highest point in the Chillingham Hills. Ros Hill is above Chillingham Castle, home to the famous herd of white cattle that has remained genetically isolated for hundreds of years. The castle is open to visitors during the summer months. See the website for more information: **http://www.chillingham-castle.com**

Cateran Rift

15m
Fell Sandstone
Map: 332 – Alnwick and Amble (although the parking place is on map 340 – Holy Island and Bamburgh)
NU 1018 2321
Easy/Moderate

Introduction
Cateran Rift is another mass-movement cave in the Fell Sandstone, situated close to the summit of Cateran Hill and logically combined with a visit to Cateran Hole. The 40m rift in which this cave is found is one of Cateran Hill's open trenches or gorges formed by vertical fractures in the sandstone, and the cave is a crawl through boulders in the floor of the rift. As this cave involves flat-out, though not difficult, crawling, it is advised that visitors wear helmets and oversuits, or at least clothing that they really, really wouldn't mind muddying and possibly tearing on the sharp rock.

Cateran Rift was first recorded by Peter Ryder of the Moldywarps Speleological Group in April 1985. He had actually set out to find Cateran Hole, having read about that cave in an 1888 guidebook written by William Weaver Tomlinson, but found this one instead. Thus did the imprecise location data of a Victorian guidebook enrich the speleological world. I can only hope that, should the unthinkable happen and it transpire that there are imperfections in this book, the speleological world will ultimately be richer for them.

The route
Most visitors will wish to combine this cave with its near neighbour Cateran Hole, so directions are given both from Cateran Hole and from the road between North Charlton and Hepburn.

If walking from Cateran Hole, follow the faint path for 150m to the bridleway heading up Cateran Hill. Turn left and follow this bridleway for 500m to the summit.

Alternatively, if visiting Cateran Rift on its own, park beside the road near Quarry House, at NU 101 246. Take the path signposted 'Public Bridleway Blawearie 2 Old Bewick 3½' for 800m and take the first left, signposted 'Public

Chris Scaife at the entrance   *Photo by Rob Scaife*

Bridleway' (NU 098 239), heading to Cateran Hill. Follow this path for 1km to the summit of Cateran Hill, with fantastic panoramic views of the northern parts of Northumberland. There is a cairn just before the summit and another at the summit.

To find Cateran Rift from the heathery summit of Cateran Hill, head west towards the distant Cheviot, and after about 230m you will reach the rocky feature of Cateran Rift, a slip trench behind the low crag, surrounded by bracken. The cave entrance is a small hole in this trench. Tread carefully in this area as the bracken can obscure some deep holes.

Towards the uphill part of the rift, there is a 4m deep hole, free-climbable with care, which may be overgrown with bracken. The entrance to the cave is a small hole facing towards this in the larger, more easily-entered part of the trench, just downhill. Crawl into the entrance and wriggle to the left, through a narrow bit, where some more wriggling through boulders leads into a chamber. At the end of the cave there is a rift, with sunlight shining through and a large boulder blocking the way out, so return and wriggle some more. This boulder is at the bottom of the 4m deep free-climbable hole, which has a separate 4m long, tight rift parallel to the one described in Cateran Rift. Of course, the boulder may at some point be removed to create a through trip.

To get back from Cateran Rift, head north on a very faint path through the heather. This path rejoins the bridleway up Cateran Hill after 360m.

Make a day of it
Combining this cave with a visit to Cateran Hole, Doubting Victoria Cave, Blawearie, Old Bewick Hillfort and Ros Castle will provide an excellent day out, packed with history, prehistory, speleology and solitude. More information on the historic sites can be found in the entry for Cateran Hole.

Doubting Victoria Cave

Length 8m
Depth 6m
Fell Sandstone
Map: 332 – Alnwick and Amble (although the parking place is on map 340 – Holy Island and Bamburgh)
NU 0899 2249
Easy

Introduction
This is a complex boulder cave in the Fell Sandstone. Although the cave and crag have been known about for years, it was first described to the caving world by Black Rose Caving Club in 2014 and takes its name from a doubter who shall remain nameless. Don Miller of Black Rose was walking and half-heartedly looking for caves with the aforementioned doubter when he espied some promising terrain in the distance. Despite his eponymous companion s protests, Don bravely persevered on foot and arrived at Dove Crags in Harehope Canyon. Here he saw that there really was a cave, so kindly returned with me one evening a few weeks later and we explored it thoroughly.

Please note that this is an important site for nesting birds, which will be particularly vulnerable between late February and early June. Please do not visit this cave at that time as disturbances may be very harmful.

The route
Although the nearest parking spot is at the tiny village of Harehope, the route described here assumes that this cave will be combined with visits to Cateran Hole and Cateran Rift, so begins at the parking place near Quarry House, at NU 101 246. Follow the path signposted 'Public Bridleway Blawearie 2 Old Bewick 3½', all the way to the abandoned cottage at Blawearie and then head due east for 600m to get into Harehope Canyon, a secluded gorge in the Fell Sandstone.

The southern entrance to the cave is beside a large overhang on the east bank of Harehope Burn. Daylight coruscates through the walls and a wide passage of stooping height leads to two exits on the northern side: one wet, one dry. A parallel flat-out 8m crawl starting at the overhang leads to another

Chris Scaife at the northern entrance   *Photo by Don Miller*

exit. By climbing up from half way along this crawl, a further chamber, 6m long, is found with an exit 6m above the floor.

Make a day of it

Combining this cave with Cateran Hole, Cateran Rift and a walk to see Blawearie, Bewick Hillfort and Ros Castle will provide an excellent day out. Additionally, the fantastic Harehope Canyon is a great place for bouldering and trad rock climbing, currently with 28 recorded routes. Following Harehope Burn south, the gorge opens out, but then narrows again after a few hundred metres, where a waterfall and another crag – Corbie Crag – is encountered. Grey Mare's Crag is immediately south of Corbie Crag and the meandering burn can be followed in more open country to a footpath at NU 089 211. This path can be followed north back to Blawearie.

Thomas Wedderburn's Hole

Length 10m
Sandstone
Map: OS Explorer Map 332 – Alnwick and Amble
NU 0770 0997
Easy

Introduction
Caves that have been known about for many years, particularly in areas where open cave entrances are few and far between, often come with grisly associated tales. This one, as far as I am aware, is to date the only cave in Northumberland to have been the scene of an execution. Thomas Wedderburn was a local reiver, cattle rustler and highwayman who hid out in this cave at the abrupt end of a lifetime of crime. The legal authorities found him here, but he refused to surrender and his reward for this impudence was to have burning oil poured into the cave entrance. He promptly exited right into the firing squad, who took aim and ended it all for him. The things people do to get caves named in their honour.

The route
Although this cave has its own signpost, this is only apparent when the cave has already been reached, so these instructions should help. The easiest way to get to Thomas Wedderburn's Hole is to park at the north-east corner of Thrunton Wood, in the small car park at NU 081 104, and follow the obvious track running west. After 600m a small path on the left leads steeply uphill. Following this path uphill for 170m you will reach a sandstone crag and a sign for Thomas Wedderburn's Hole. The letters TW are clearly visible, inscribed into the rock at the entrance.

    Crawl down into the entrance. Immediately on the left is a small chamber. Once through the brief crawl, enter a standing height rift 6m long. At the end of the rift is a jumble of rocks and a couple of holes in the floor leading into tiny chambers. At this end of the rift, it is possible to exit the cave through a gap at chest height.

TW inscription at the entrance

Make a day of it

Thrunton Wood is a very interesting place, well worth exploring further. There are some other short caves worth visiting, as well as the site of an Iron Age fort. There are two waymarked trails running through the woodland: the Crag Top Walk, marked in green, is roughly 3km; and the Castle Hill Walk, marked in red, is about 6km. Thrunton Wood contains plenty of other paths and is also an excellent spot for mountain biking, although the mountain biking trails are not currently waymarked. The route described here follows the red walking route fairly closely, with some worthwhile detours to see an Iron Age fort and two tiny caves.

Having visited Thomas Wedderburn's Hole, head back downhill on the small path to rejoin the large track. Turn left and follow this track south-west for about 1km. After the path bends to the right there is a large pond on the left. Take the sharp right turn here and continue on the red route towards Humbleton Hill. Follow this obvious track down, ignoring any paths off to the side, to get to the northern edge of the wood, where the track turns left.

Continue on the main track as it skirts the northern edge of the forest and then take the obvious track on the left heading south to Castle Hill. At NU 063 097 go through the gate in the wall on the right-hand side of the track.

Follow the path on the left to the top of Castle Hill. This is the site of an Iron Age fort and some fantastic gnarled beech trees, a place to be savoured. To proceed, follow the path south, initially with small rock faces on either side. This path winds downhill, then crosses over a stile, before leading steeply up to the man-made Macartney's Cave, at NU 0608 0938. This interesting sacerdotal feature, 2.5m long and 1.9m high, was hand-crafted by a 19th century monk from nearby Callaly, and used as a solitary retreat. It is sometimes also known as Priest's Cave.

Continuing uphill and slightly to the left leads to a large, impressive arch formed by several smaller boulders wedged over two massive boulders. Keep going uphill to the plateau at the crest of Hard Nab. Where the small uphill path joins this ridge, there is a prehistoric cairn. Another, larger, cairn can be found by following the path to the right a short distance.

From the crest, take the path to the left, east, which soon leaves the forest for a short section on the open moor. Go through the gate in the dry stone wall at NU 063 091 and follow the track right for 50m, then take a sharp left onto the large track. This track passes Callaly Crag on the left-hand side and has a few viewpoints offering magnificent views to the north. Continue along this track for 1.5km. About 200m after a sign indicating both red and green walking routes on the right, there is a small path on the left, which passes a bench and leads to a 3m cave at NU 0771 0992, which can be entered through a small hole in the ground. Although this small cave is very close to Thomas Wedderburn's Hole, the terrain in the area is rather awkward, so it is best to return along the red route.

Go back to the junction where the red and green trails are marked and follow the red trail back towards the main car park. At NU 084 097, follow the track left, which goes up, then down, then around a left-hand turn. Immediately after this turn, take the small path to the right (in effect straight ahead). This path heads downhill to the edge of the wood, then joins a large track going back to the car park.

Coe Crag Cave

5m
Fell Sandstone
Map: 332 – Alnwick and Amble
NU 0725 0724
Moderate

Introduction
This cave is something of a novelty as it is located quite high up a crag, thus it is only accessible by either rock climbing from below or abseiling in from above.

The north-facing Coe Crag, at the southern end of Thrunton Wood, has been known to climbers for many years. This crag is composed of three main buttresses: Raven's Buttress (sadly no longer home to nesting ravens), Cave Buttress (happily still home to a cave) and Neb Buttress (identified by the large neb, or nose of rock). Cave Buttress is approximately 15m in height and so named because a rather capacious cavity dominates the face at a height of about 5m.

Cave Buttress

Please be courteous to others in the wood and at the crag. Mountain biking is quite popular here and it is generally easiest and safest for those on foot to get out of the way of those on bikes. If planning to abseil down the buttress, first check that there is nobody climbing up it.

Although it is assumed that the cave had been entered prior to this, the first recorded ascent of Cave Buttress is by climbers Dave Roberts and Allan Austin in 1968.

The route
Cars can be parked beside the road at Rough Castles, NU 092 072, where a forestry road heads into the woods. Rough Castles is 200m along the minor road to Thrunton Wood, which forks off from the A697 about 800m north of the crossroads with the B6341. Follow the large track into the woodland for about 1km to a clearing. Just before the power lines, take a small path to the right, which starts downhill, then goes under the power lines and into the forest, on a broad path that is not obvious until you get close. About 150m along this broad path, there is a fork in the track. Left leads uphill, but the best path to follow is to the right. After 500m there is another junction. Head left, uphill.

It is now 1km to the top of the hill, along a path that soon emerges onto open moorland. There is a cairn at the top of the hill and the crag is reached a short distance farther on. Walk downhill to the right to get to the foot of the crag. The first large buttress you will reach is Raven's Buttress and right next to that is Cave Buttress. There are several classic rock climbs, ranging from Mild Severe to E2 5b, that ascend this buttress and can be used to get to the cave. Alternatively, if abseiling in, there is a very large boulder above the buttress that can be used as an anchor for the rope. A minimum 30m rope is recommended for the descent.

The cave entrance is 7m wide and averages about 1m high. The floor is quite soft and the unobstructed views to the north are glorious.

Make a day of it
The intricacies of this crag make it a place worth exploring. There are numerous small voids in the crag walls and under boulders. Those interested in climbing will find plenty of entertaining rock at Coe Crag, whether it be the routes on the main buttresses or bouldering on the smaller outcrops nearby. There are also mountain biking trails throughout the woodland, though these are not currently waymarked. See the entry for Thomas Wedderburn's Hole for a walking tour of the northern part of Thrunton Wood.

Pupienus Hole

7m
Fell Sandstone
Map: 332 – Alnwick and Amble
NU 1259 0974
Easy

Introduction

This small boulder cave may well have been known about for centuries, as it is situated on a steep hillside close to an extensive Iron Age settlement. It remained, however, unknown to the speleological world until it was spotted, but not entered, in November 2015 by Don Miller of Black Rose Caving Club, on an impromptu trip into some woods by the road when driving home from Alnwick. He very kindly took me to see, and enter, the cave in June 2016.

As Don Miller is a Roman historian, the cave was named after one of his favourite historical figures. Pupienus Maximus was Roman Emperor for just three months in 238, during the Year of the Six Emperors.

Both the walk and the cave are only very short and a visit is unlikely to occupy much time in its own right. Fortunately, it is located in such a position that it can easily be visited very quickly when travelling by road between Alnwick and Rothbury.

The route

Park at NU 126 098 in a small lay-by beside the stone Corby's Bridge, which crosses the stream known as Corby's Letch, 7km from Alnwick on the B6341 between Alnwick and Rothbury. A pleasant waterfall is visible upstream from this bridge.

Walk steeply uphill to the right, through the birch trees. The cave is within some large boulders about 50m due south of the road bridge.

Pupienus Hole is a flat-floored stooping-height passage formed by the large boulders on each side. It is best entered through the larger north entrance. There is a small hole at the southern end, which can be used as an exit squeeze. A hole in the ceiling just before this exit squeeze provides a short, entertaining scramble.

Pupienus Hole

Make a day of it

Pupienus Hole is located very close to the main road between Alnwick and Rothbury and, as such, can easily be visited by anyone driving, or cycling, between these two towns. Both are described in more detail in the entries for Nine Year Aud Hole and Ward's Hill Quarry Caves respectively.

It is worth taking a look at the Iron Age settlement while you are here, and this is found by heading uphill a short distance, to where the slope levels out. Corby's Crags rock shelter, at NU 1280 0965, is found further up the hill and is a natural overhang on the crag with evidence of prehistoric activity. Excavations carried out here in 1975 found Mesolithic flints and a vessel containing the remains of a Bronze Age cremation.

The small but elegant Edlingham Castle, in the care of English Heritage but with free entry, can be visited by following the B6341 south-east from the lay-by and taking the right-hand turn after 1.3km. The castle is accessed through the churchyard of the delightful 11th century St John the Baptist Church.

Nine Year Aud Hole

12m
Sandstone
Map: 332 – Alnwick and Amble
NU 1570 1458
Easy

Introduction

Nine Year Aud Hole is an interesting and straightforward cave, reached by a pleasant walk. The cave has been formed by the mass movement of sandstone on a steep crag in Hulne Park, just outside the market town of Alnwick. Hulne Park is the former hunting ground of the Duke of Northumberland, who resides at Alnwick Castle. It has belonged to the Percy family since 1309, when Lord Henry Percy purchased the castle and the Barony of Alnwick. At the end of the Middle Ages there were nearly 1,000 hapless deer in the park, all awaiting cervicide by sporting nobles. The park is usually open to the public between 11am and sunset each day, and dogs are not permitted. To check for closures, call the Estate Office on 01665 510777.

One of the highlights of Hulne Park is Brizlee Tower, a 26m Gothick tower commissioned in 1777 to commemorate Lady Elizabeth Seymour, the wife of Hugh Percy, Duke of Northumberland. This folly tower was designed by architect Robert Adam and built by local

Stone friar guarding Nine Year Aud Hole

mason Matthew Mills. Portraits of the Duke and Duchess can be seen in roundels on the exterior.

Outside the cave there is a late 18th century statue of a robed, bearded Carmelite, or 'White Friar'. This is similar to the stone statues found at Hulne Friary.

The route

Park in Alnwick beside the road near the grand gatehouse entrance to Hulne Park, NU 180 137. The walk from here is mostly along a tarmac road; however only authorised vehicles may drive in Hulne Park.

Follow the road into the park. After 600m you will cross a bridge and after another 200m the road splits. Right leads to a sawmill but continue along the road, Farm Drive, signposted 'Park Farm House'. Another 1km from this junction the road splits again, with right leading to Percy Farms and Park Farm; again, continue straight ahead on Farm Road and after 300m turn left, uphill, onto a loose, gravelly road.

Follow this track for 1.3km, ignoring any paths off to either side. At NU 158 147 (500m along this gravelly track) Brizlee Tower is seen on the right-hand side, and 400m further on from this is a walled garden, built as a burial site for the Duke of Northumberland. About 150m from this walled garden, turn left at a crossroads and after a further 150m the stone friar to the left guards the entrance to the cave.

Enter the cave via the small eastern entrance up and to the right of a large slab, on which an Yggdrasilian beech tree has spread its roots. Walk in for 4m, then drop through a small hole in the floor. The cave then enlarges and exit can be made through the very wide western entrance, with a large rocky overhang to the right and dense foliage to the left.

After exploring the cave, turn left and continue along this track, which soon rejoins the gravelly road. There is now a pleasant return journey to the park's entrance.

Make a day of it

There are three waymarked trails in Hulne Park and the route to the cave covers, more or less, the 6.4km yellow trail. To see more of the park, the 10km blue trail is the best route to take. This can be joined at the end of the gravelly road leading back from the cave. When this gravelly road reaches Farm Road, to continue along the blue trail turn left. Farm Road sweeps around and crosses the River Aln by East Brizlee Bridge, then leads to Hulne Friary. This 13th century friary, often erroneously referred to as Hulne Abbey, but occupied by friars rather than monks, was founded by the Carmelites, who apparently chose this site because of its resemblance to Mount Carmel near Israel's Mediterranean coast, where the order was founded. The eagle-eyed will find several more stone friars in the grounds here. The blue trail stays close to the Aln all the way back to the park entrance.

Alnwick is a very interesting town with much to offer. The most popular visitor attractions are Alnwick Castle and Alnwick Garden. The castle has been the home of the Percy family, the Earls and Dukes of Northumberland, since 1309. With its strategic position so close to the border between England and Scotland, the castle has a colourful history. As one of the best preserved medieval castles in the country, it is often used as a filming location, so may be familiar as the home of the Black Adder himself, as well as the setting for Hogwarts in the first Harry Potter film.

One of the country's largest second-hand bookshops, Barter Books, is housed in the Victorian Alnwick Station building. This marvellous place contains thousands of books of great variety, and a cosy café in the former waiting room. It was in this shop that the original Second World War poster, 'Keep Calm and Carry On' was found, in a box of old books, in 2000.

THE HEART OF THE COUNTY

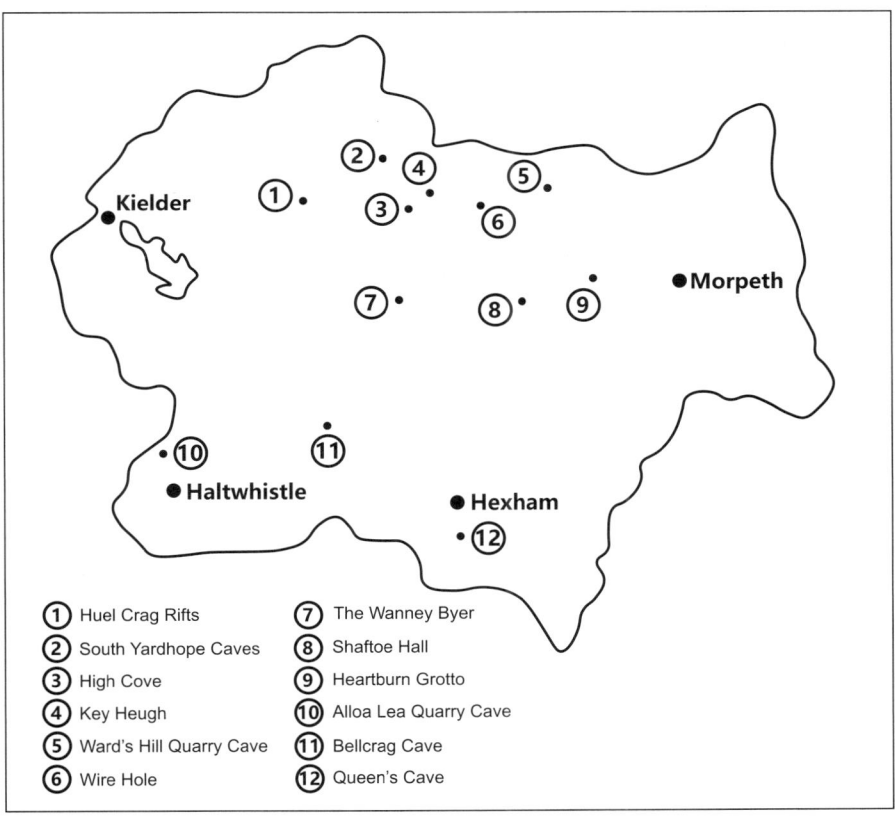

Cave locations in the Heart of the County

Among the notable features of the large area of land between the River Coquet in the north, and the River Tyne in the south, are the enormous plantation of Kielder Forest and the great Roman structure of Hadrian's Wall.

Kielder Forest is a vast expanse of woodland, which surrounds Kielder village and the largest man-made lake in northern Europe, Kielder Water. The forest

Chris Scaife in Wark Forest, by the entrance to Bellcrag Cave
Photo by Carolina Smith de la Fuente

offers excellent mountain biking and walking, with some of the most remote hilltops in England. Kielder Forest is also home to more bothies than anywhere else in England. These remote mountain huts offer shelter in the wildest places in the UK. For more information about bothies, or to join the Mountain Bothies Association, see the website: **https://www.mountainbothies.org.uk/**

There can be few historical sites in the UK as important as Hadrian's Wall. This Roman wall was declared a UNESCO World Heritage Site in 1987 and is one of the most popular ancient tourist attractions in the country. Those wishing to see all the settlements, turrets and forts should consider Hadrian's Wall Path, a 135km (84 miles) long distance walk from Bowness-on-Solway to Wallsend.

Most of the caves in the heart of the county are formed in sandstone and suitable for beginners without caving gear, but there are a couple of more challenging caves in limestone. There is surface limestone in a few places in this region, notably south of Rothbury and in the area around Wark Forest.

Ward's Hill Quarry Caves and Wire Hole are the only known caves in the limestone near Rothbury, although shakeholes and karstic features are noted at several sites nearby. To date, Bellcrag Cave is the only limestone cave to have been explored in Wark Forest, but there may be other caves here secreted away, and indeed there are some shakeholes emitting draughts.

The water flowing out from nearby Grindon Lough, which lies between limestone ridges at NY 805 677, flows north along the Knag Burn, then into a small cave which sumps almost immediately. This flooded passage has not been entered, but it appears that the water continues underground for some considerable distance, with the presumed resurgence being small springs near Vindolanda, 3km away to the south-west. Fanciful perhaps, but it is possible that a tremendous cave system lies beneath, waiting to be explored.

Huel Crag Rifts

Three caves with lengths up to 34m
Fell Sandstone
Map: OL42 – Kielder Water and Forest
NY 8292 9951 to NY 8290 9955
Easy/Moderate

Introduction
Huel Crag in Redesdale is a fantastic place, where huge boulders, rifts and scars poke through the birch, lichen and moss to give the appearance of a lost world. Rock climbing started here in the 1960s, with Gordon Thompson climbing several routes, some of which were inside the crag. In 1985, Peter Ryder of the Moldywarps Speleological Group, having read in a climbing guidebook about this locally rare opportunity for underground climbing, went to investigate, and recorded three caves of a respectable length.

Warning – Close to the military firing range at Otterburn Training Area. If the sublunary forces are using their big guns, these placid grottos may be transformed into reverberating dens of horror. To avoid unnecessary quaking and, perhaps, reduce laundry bills, I would suggest that you check to see if there will be any military training before you go. Firing times are currently displayed at **https://www.gov.uk/government/publications/otterburn-firing-times**

The route
Park in the lay-by at NY 833 985, near Bremenium Roman Fort, on the minor road that runs north from the A68 at Rochester. The footpath is a short distance uphill from the lay-by. Head left on a public footpath that seems to go through somebody's garden, and follow the path downwards, crossing a small stream via a wooden bridge. Two pleasant waterfalls can be viewed by taking a very short detour up this stream. Get back onto the footpath and follow this to a small group of conifers at the corner of the wood (NY 828 994), then follow the fence uphill to the gate. Go through this gate and continue uphill to Huel Crag. The three main caves are described starting from this southern edge of the crag. There are several other shorter caves in the

maze of boulders and it is certainly worth exploring this area thoroughly when you visit.

Huel Crag Rift 1
34m
NY 8292 9951

Just below the top of the crag is this complex cave, which has four entrances at the uphill end. These entrances are progressively easier heading north, with the southernmost entrance a thrutchy squeeze and the northernmost a simple walk. All four entrances unite in a 6m high rift, with several daylight holes above. A downward passage to the left curves around to the right, reaching a dead end with a healthy population of cave spiders. Back in the rift, a climb up leads to two very tight perpendicular rifts. These are both a few metres long, but only thin cavers will get far. On the left, a short climb up and easy squeeze completes the through trip.

Huel Crag Rift 2
15m
NY 8290 9952

This rift, 10m high, gives an easy through trip if staying at floor level. The obvious entrance is just a short distance north of Rift 1 and is a tall, narrow crack beside a tower of rock that juts out towards the heavens. In wet weather there may be a large pool of water at the southern end, but ledges above this can be used to traverse higher. It is possible, with care, to climb to the top of the rift, where there are several exits and an impressive wide section. The rock is loose and slippery at the top of the rift, so take great care if attempting any traversing at this height. Just around the corner, a few metres east of the exit of this rift at floor level, is Rift 3.

Huel Crag Rift 3
21m
NY 8290 9955

A crawl down leads into a walking passage, 12m long. Several small rifts head off in various directions. Before reaching the back of the cave, a 4m climb up on the left leads into a large walking passage heading back into daylight after 5m.

Make a day of it
The moss-draped birches and dramatic rock formations at Huel Crag may beguile many hours for the aesthetes amongst us, but for the rover in us all

Chris Scaife in Huel Crag Rift 3　　　　　　　　*Photo by Don Miller*

there is more to see nearby. The remains of Bremenium Roman Fort encircle the minor road at the point where the footpath is taken from the road towards Huel Crag, NY 833 986, and it is worth a wander around this site. There is a path all around the perimeter of the fort, measuring about 700m in total. Bremenium, far to the north of Hadrian's Wall, was an important defensive structure along Dere Street, the Roman road that ran north from York at least as far as the Antonine Wall in what is now the Central Belt of Scotland.

Brigantium, NY 829 981, which was formerly a replica Iron Age roundhouse, has now been converted into an amphitheatre called Rochester Roundhouse, which occasionally hosts activities and events. This attraction can be reached by a permissive footpath that runs from the south-west corner of Bremenium Roman Fort.

South Yardhope Caves

Four caves with lengths up to 21m
Fell Sandstone
Map: OL 42 – Kielder Water and Forest
NT 9248 0056 to NT 9244 0049
Easy

Introduction
South Yardhope Crag has been known to rock climbers for decades, with many climbing routes receiving first ascents in the 1970s. The *Northumberland Climbing Guide* mentions 'some interesting caves where a small stream flows through the crag'. No further details were available, so in 2017 I went to investigate, accompanied by Carolina Smith de la Fuente of Black Rose Caving Club.

This is on the Ministry of Defence firing range, so stay away if the red flag is flying, although at all other times there are no access issues. Even the approach road is out of bounds at times of live firing. Firing times for the Otterburn Training Area are currently displayed at **https://www.gov.uk/government/publications/otterburn-firing-times**

The caves here are formed by a number of large boulders lying across the stream and can be used to make an entertaining journey up the hill. The first three caves are very close together, with one leading immediately on to the next.

The route
The best approach is to leave the B6341 Elsdon to Rothbury road at Billsmoorfoot and follow the single-track military road for about 5km until South Yardhope Crag is visible on the left. There are several parking areas beside the road. Walk along the road to where the Rowantree Cleugh passes through a culvert, at NT 925 009. There are rowan trees beside the stream, as the name suggests. Follow this stream uphill to the south for 400m until you find boulders lying across the stream.

South Yardhope Lower Cave
3m
NT 9248 0056

The first boulder lying across the Rowantree Cleugh provides a 3m long flat-out crawl, with a rising squeeze at the upstream end, which may require some excavation. Anyone who cannot fit through this squeeze can return and walk around the side of the boulder to get to the next cave.

South Yardhope Main Cave
21m
NT 9248 0055

After emerging from, or walking around, the Lower Cave, you will find a much larger boulder upstream. Crawling under this is the start of a 21m underground journey. Follow the stream, flat-out, for 6m, then take a left turn followed by a right turn and continue upstream into an impressive chamber, 7m long and 8m wide, with a 2.5m waterfall.

South Yardhope Rock Shelter
6m
NT 9247 0053

There is a spacious rock shelter beside the stream above the Main Cave.

Although it is possible to climb up the waterfall in the Main Cave, this is quite unpleasant so most people will choose to walk around. Take care in this area though, as there are some deep holes that are well concealed by vegetation. The rock shelter has several openings, and its dimensions are 6m x 4.5m x 4m high.

Waterfall inside South Yardhope Main Cave

South Yardhope Upper Cave
4m
NT 9244 0049

About 50m upstream of the rock shelter, there is a short section with steep, rocky sides. At the downstream end of this rocky section, beside a small natural arch, there is a short boulder cave that offers another through trip.

Make a day of it
There is a very interesting Romano-British shrine close to the caves, amongst boulders about 50m east of the rock shelter, at NT 9252 0053. This rectangular structure is an excellent example of the Celtic-style places of veneration that were found on the fringes of the Roman Empire, still heavily influenced by pre-Roman traditions. It is roughly 2m square and up to 2m high. On the rock face at the entrance is a fine carved figure of the local deity Cocidius.

There is a 'Rob Roy's Cave' marked on the OS map at NT 9467 0244, but this is a fairly uninteresting rock shelter on private land and is not worth a visit. The nearby Holystone Wood, however, is certainly worth a visit and contains a number of unmarked walking trails.

HIGH COVE

Eight caves with lengths up to 16m
Depths up to 6m
Sandstone
Map: OL 42 – Kielder Water and Forest
NY 9519 9583 to NY 9513 9571
Easy to Moderate

Introduction

High Cove, also occasionally known as Carrow Rigg Gash, is a major sandstone slip feature running more or less from north to south. At its northern end, High Cove is a composite of narrow rifts and boulders. The complex nature of the place means that there are numerous short caves, holes and trenches. However, I have identified eight caves of particular note. Keep an eye on the ground beneath your feet in this area as there are many loose rocks and some holes in the ground may be much deeper than they look. This is close to the Otterburn Training Area, but not actually on it, so you might hear some loud bangs but are unlikely to get blown up. Most of these caves involve mud or water and some element of touching the walls, so oversuits and wellies are recommended.

Four caves were explored, but not named, by Peter Ryder of the Moldywarps Speleological Group in April 1985. The other caves were first recorded when I visited with Don Miller of Black Rose Caving Club on the 1st of April 2015. Perhaps there is something about this place that attracts exploration in April and years in which Back to the Future films have been set. On the other hand, it could just be an amazing coincidence.

The route

There is a fairly large lay-by at NY 939 956, 2km north of Elsdon on the B6341. Go through the gate and follow the large wall heading downhill. Looking east, as you head downhill, the grassy area in the distance, on the far side of Park Burn, contains two thin horizontal strips of heather to the right of the wall. The lower of these is the much shallower Low Cove and the higher is High Cove. It is best to follow the wall from the car park, go through the gate after

500m, then after fighting your way through the gorse, stay as close as possible to the wall, crossing Park Burn wherever you can, and then turn right to walk across to High Cove, leaving the wall behind roughly 1.4km from the car park. The holly tree, and nearby birch tree, marking Holly Tree Hole, should be obvious. The trees won't last forever though, so if you're reading this in an even more deforested distant future, I can only apologise for my myopic reliance on such evanescent landmarks.

Holly Tree Hole
Length 15m
Depth 4m
NY 9519 9583

The entrance is a hole 7m long, 2m wide and 4m deep, with a distinctive holly tree. Climb down the south-western end of the hole into a daylight shaft. At the far end of this shaft, 3m of walking through water leads to a squeeze on the left into 5m of narrow passage, standing height with knee-deep water.

Chris Scaife in Holly Tree Hole *Photo by Don Miller*

April Fools' Cave
Length 13m
Depth 3m
NY 9520 9584

A small hole 15m east of Holly Tree Hole drops down 3m, followed by 4.5m walking passage to the first squeeze – best tackled at waist-height. This is shortly followed by another squeeze, Poisson d'avril, tackled at floor level. The passage then continues around a left-hand bend.

Des Pot
Depth 6m
NY 9517 9582

A hole 18m south-west of Holly Tree Hole is this interesting, mossy-walled pot, which can be free-climbed with care.

Cruciform Rift
Length 12m
Depth 5m
NY 9516 9580

South of Des Pot, this rift can be reached by an entertaining through trip in a trench. A 5m climb down a narrow slit, with loose rocks, leads into a rift 7.5m long. Towards the deepest point is a perpendicular rift of 4.5m.

Sandstone Stream Cave
11m
NY 9515 9579

A narrow rift heading north, with vertical sandstone slabs on either side. A mossy entrance is followed by a stooping rift, with a clamber over boulders leading into the final chamber. A rivulet flows through this chamber – a rare sight in Northumberland sandstone caves.

Overhang Hole
Length 7m
Depth 5m
NY 9514 9578

Under a large, bracken-covered overhang facing south-east. The hole beneath the overhang leads into a large chamber, with a rift heading south. Daylight enters from above the end farthest from the entrance.

High Cove Main Cave
16m
NY 9513 9574

Towards the southern end of High Cove, the landscape changes from a maze of boulders, rifts and trenches to a more uniform, square-shaped valley. A small hole low down on the western wall leads down into this large rift, running northwards, with a vertical left wall and a slanting right wall. This is walking passage until just before the end, where a short crawl is needed to reach the farthest extremity. There is a small upper entrance, which leads into a short upper passage.

Capreolus Cavern
10m
NY 9513 9571

Almost at the end of High Cove now, a small path enters on the western side. Just below this path is a large boulder jutting out. An easy triangular squeeze under this boulder leads into a large chamber followed by a mixture of walking and stooping to reach the end. This cave gets its name from a dead buck roe deer we found at the entrance.

Make a day of it

Exploring High Cove fully is likely to take a fair few hours and on a clear day this is a marvellous place to be. Nearby Low Cove has less speleological interest, but is still worth seeing, with many large boulders perched in strange positions.

The summit of Darden Pike at NY 968 955 offers excellent views of the heather moorland and can be reached by following the fence above High Cove, south-east to NY 959 954, where another fence is met, which heads east towards the trig point. Just 300m beyond Darden Pike is the tranquil tarn of Darden Lough.

The picturesque village of Elsdon is 2km south of the recommended parking place and is certainly worth visiting, with its large village green and several interesting historic buildings. At NY 938 935 the earthwork of the 11th century Elsdon Castle, 80m wide and 15m high, is widely regarded as the best example of a motte-and-bailey castle in Northumberland. On the other side of the burn is the medieval Elsdon Tower, a vicar's pele tower that was restored in the 1990s. St Cuthbert's Church in Elsdon is also worth a visit. Most of the present building is from the 14th century, but investigations using geophysics have suggested that there may be the site of an earlier church in the green just north of the churchyard. This gives a shred of evidence to the tradition that this church was one of the resting places of the monks transporting the relics of Saint Cuthbert.

Key Heugh Caves

Numerous small caves with lengths up to 8m
Depths up to 5m
Fell Sandstone
Map: OL 42 – Kielder Water and Forest
NY 9670 9714 to NY 9683 9711
Easy

Introduction
The large west-facing crag Key Heugh, also known as Sandy Crag – but not to be confused with a collection of boulders 1km to the east, known as Sandy Crags – ascends to a height of 20m and has been known to rock climbers since the 1950s, with currently about 40 routes graded from Moderate to E7. Climbing opportunities, of course, pale into significance when there is the chance to get underground. I first inspected this area late in the summer of 2017, hoping to find caves to compare with those at nearby High Cove.

This is an extraordinarily complex landscape, rife with small boulder caves scattered across a wide area. The heather, bilberries and bracken are often very dense, making entrances difficult to spot, so any attempt to catalogue precise locations of every single cave in this area would be likely to confuse rather than help. Instead I have described how to get to the area with the caves, described the locations of one or two interesting features that should be quite easy to find, and left further exploration to my bold readers.

Please note that this crag is an important nesting site for birds, so to avoid disturbance it is best not to visit between late February and early June. Also, be aware that this is an active grouse shooting moor, so if visiting after the Glorious Twelfth try not to get shot.

The route
Park at the picnic site off the B6341, between Elsdon and Hepple, at NY 970 994. Follow the road south, then by the bridge take the track towards Midgy Ha, reaching this cottage after 1km. From Midgy Ha, follow the stream south for about another 1km towards the Humble Law plantation and the impressive crag of Key Heugh should be clearly visible from here. Cross the open fell, over tough terrain, towards the crag.

En route to the crag, there are numerous large boulders that provide rock shelters and small caves, all worthy of inspection. Of note are the following caves, although there are many others, and indeed there may be some larger ones that I have missed:

Key Heugh Cave 1
5m long, 6m wide
NY 9670 9714

This boulder cave is found in a depression 20m north of a prominent, heathery outcrop of rock.

Key Heugh Cave 2
5m
NY 9677 9721

A crawling rift under a large slab, towards the northern part of the crag.

Key Heugh Cave 3
5m deep
NY 9679 9720

Not far from Cave 2, this is a mossy, free-climbable hole. Just a few metres south, there is a 4m deep climb through large, flat, slanting boulders, which is open at both ends.

Key Heugh Crag

Key Heugh Cave 4
8m
NY 9685 9720

This one is very close to the main crag. Clamber over boulders into a fairly roomy void. This cave is complex, with several openings.

Key Heugh Cave 5
7m
NY 9683 9711

Below the southernmost point of the main crag, in a shallow but well-defined valley running south-west. Stoop under a boulder and go left. The roof soon lowers to a flat-out crawl.

There is also an interesting trench just below the main crag, at NY 9686 9718. This is 8m long, open-roofed, 1m wide and up to about 3m high. It is a very curious feature, which looks as though it belongs under the sea.

Make a day of it

Exploring every nook and cranny in this area could easily take more than a full day. However, anyone looking for an enjoyable walk, or fell run, should follow the waymarked path from the lay-by off the B6341 at NY 959 981. This very pleasant 7km circuit will take you across Miller's Moss to the 374m summit of Darden Pike and past the tarn of Darden Lough.

Ward's Hill Quarry Caves

Three caves with lengths up to 120m
Quarried limestone
Map: OL 42 – Kielder Water and Forest
NZ 0795 9660 to NZ 0791 9656
Moderate/Difficult

Introduction
There are three caves in this disused limestone quarry, which is about 6km south of Rothbury. All are narrow, clay-floored phreatic passages. They are muddy and involve flat-out crawling for most of their lengths, with a few squeezes. Owing to these difficulties they are not recommended for inexperienced cavers.

Ward's Hill Quarry is of interest to geologists as a rare example of a site where the Lower Carboniferous limestone and shale is intruded with Whin Sill. It was used for fieldwork by the Newcastle University Geology Department and in 1976, whilst studying the Whin Sill exposure, Mike Ridealgh observed three cave entrances. He wrote a letter, as was customary at the time, to the Moldywarps Speleological Group, whose members Peter Ryder, John Habershon and Chris Langthorne went to investigate the North Cave and the Main System over several visits. There have been some clandestine extensions in both of these caves since this time, and the North-East Cave, which was identified by the original explorers only as a 'choked entrance' has been dug out and pushed a short distance. The identity of these latter-day explorers remains a mystery.

The route
Cars can be parked at NZ 078 965 on a flat, grassy patch beside the minor road that runs south-west from Embleton Terrace. Follow the grassy track east into the round quarry. Directly ahead, just 200m from the parking spot, is a curved band of shale. At the base of this is the very low entrance to the first cave.

Ward's Hill Quarry North-East Cave
9m
NZ 0795 9660

A flat-out entrance squeeze below the band of shale may require some excavation. The passage heads left, briefly parallel to the quarry face, then turns right, flat-out all the way. After 9m there is a junction, with short passages leading off to the right and sharply to the left. At present these are blocked with clay at floor level. Removal of some of this clay would no doubt increase the length of navigable passage, but the length potential is unlikely to be great.

From the North-East Cave, head south-west. Entrances to the North Cave and the Main Cave are in the first rocky band on the right-hand side, just below the track used to enter the quarry. Both have small entrances, which may be blocked up by piles of stones.

Ward's Hill Quarry North Cave
30m
NZ 0792 9657

Through the narrow entrance there is a short slope down to the right, followed by a short slope up. Straight ahead soon chokes but to the left there is a small void. On the right in this void there are now a couple of rising squeezes, leading into passage going around a corner into what would in most caves be considered a crawl, but in this quarry should be celebrated as a chamber. Several very short choked passages lead off, and a narrow squeeze on the right, opposite a 3m side-passage, leads into a flat-out crawl. This continues as a short struggle for about 6m to a dead end, completely blocked with clay.

Ward's Hill Quarry Main Cave
120m
NZ 0791 9656

The entrance is in the same rocky band, 20m south-west of the North Cave. A narrow slope leads down into the Main Chamber, which is crawling-

Entrance to Ward's Hill Quarry Main Cave

height only. Straight ahead, a crawl leads to a section that is too tight, but beyond looks to continue for a short distance. Up a muddy slope leads into the almost spacious Warren of Gummy Bunnies, which is so named because evidence of lagomorph habitation is rife. The passage on from here bends to the right and the clay floor soon gets quite muddy. A short slope down to the right from this clay mire leads into a choked bedding chamber, whilst to the left is also choked, but straight ahead continues as a narrow, tenebrous crawl to a muddy slope, which is blocked with clay at the top. This extension from the clay mire is something of a double-edged sword – on the one hand it has increased the length of the cave, but on the other it does rather eliminate any hopes of cleanliness.

On the opposite side of the Main Chamber there is a choice of three passages. The first one on the left, if returning from the Warren of Gummy Bunnies, is a short passage to a small hole up into a slightly larger passage. A little further along the Main Chamber is a passage which immediately splits into two – to the right is a tubular crawl and on the left a short connection with the first one. These all soon unite in a small chamber and lead past a tube on the right, to a now thoroughly blocked former entrance, into a short, flat-out crawl, which soon reaches a choke past a large block.

Make a day of it

Simonside Ridge Walk is a very pleasant nearby waymarked 6km walking trail, which combines woodland with the sweeping vistas of the Simonside Hills. The route is easy to follow from the parking area, and picnic spot, at NZ 037 997. A very small cave, known as Little Church Cave, is reached by a short detour en route and is said to have been a hiding place of the legendary Simonside Dwarfs, or Duergar, who led travellers astray on dark nights, sometimes to their doom. On a clear day there are impressive views along the ridge from the 430m summit of Simonside. There is a rock shelter not far from the summit, as well as several more very small caves within the crag and in jumbles of boulders along the ridge.

The market town of Rothbury, the 'Capital of Coquetdale', is very picturesque and worth a visit for its independent shops, pubs and art galleries. It is also a starting point for many interesting walks and bike rides. The National Trust property at Cragside was the Victorian country retreat of the first Lord Armstrong - a northeasterner of great importance in the Industrial Age and the first engineer to be ennobled. This was the first house in the world to be lit by hydroelectric power. Visitors today can explore the woodland and gardens, as well as seeing the opulent house and hydraulic contraptions. The existence of such technology using renewable energy so long ago brings shame on our current unsustainable dependence on fossil fuels and deforestation.

More information about Cragside can be found at:
https://www.nationaltrust.org.uk/cragside

Wire Hole

Length 6m
Depth 8m
Limestone
Map: OL 42 – Kielder Water and Forest
NZ 0407 9265
Moderate

Introduction
I first went to look for caves in the limestone around Greenleighton Quarry in December 2016 with Carolina Smith de la Fuente. Having seen that there was a disused limestone quarry with several shakeholes marked nearby on the Ordnance Survey map, we were hopeful that we might find some caves. In the walls of the quarry, we found a cornucopia of holes that were not quite big enough to be considered caves, with several rifts and tiny phreatic tubes. Running downhill from the top of the quarry we found a line of shakeholes that led towards a fenced-off group of trees containing the most promising

The gentle slopes of Greenleighton Hill

shakehole, but also the most dreadful. Amongst these trees was a hole that had been used to dump coils and coils of rusty wire, but which probably had a cave lurking underneath, just waiting to be unearthed by a keen digger, or at least a keen wire-coil-mover, with adequate tetanus vaccination.

A year later, I was staying at a caving hut in the Yorkshire Dales when David Keegan from the University of Newcastle Caving Club told me he was keen on looking for caves and asked me if I could suggest anywhere he might find something. I showed him my photos of the shakeholes up near Greenleighton Quarry and he seemed far more enthusiastic about digging through scrap metal than I had ever been. David made a few trips up to look at the shakeholes and said he had managed to get underground in one of them, then in September 2018 Carolina and I accompanied him to look at this glorious find and explore it to the bitter end.

Please note that this cave has been used for the tipping of a large quantity of rusty wire. This has made the cave a very loose and dangerous place, so a descent is not recommended. Frankly, unless you are writing a guidebook to the caves of Northumberland there is little to be gained from entering this cave. Perhaps in the future this situation will change; if there was none of the rubbish in there, this would be a nice little pothole.

The route

Cars can be parked in the National Trust car park for Greenleighton Quarry, at NZ 035 915. Follow the path up Greenleighton Hill, with the disused limestone quarry on your right. After passing the trig point, a height of 284m, continue to the corner of the fence, at the north-western corner of Greenleighton Quarry. Now turn right and follow the fence around the edge of the quarry for about 300m, until you reach a shallow, dry valley heading gently downhill. Follow this dry valley, which contains a line of shakeholes, for 600m to a fenced-off group of trees.

The cave entrance is, at present, mostly obscured by large coils of wire. If you are able to find a way through the wire you will arrive in a fairly spacious chamber. There are a few tiny stalactites for the observant. Looking up you will see that the ceiling is not made of solid rock, but from the coils of wire. The bottom of the cave can be reached by climbing down over loose rock, but then you will no doubt want to get out as fast as your legs will carry you, in order to avoid a most awful burial.

Make a day of it

The waymarked Greenleighton Moor walk is an enjoyable 6 mile (9.6km) circular walk, which passes the shakeholes. From Wire Hole, continue gently downhill across moorland to NZ 045 928, then go north to Fontburn Reservoir. Now go left along the southern edge of the reservoir, through mixed woodland. At the western end of the reservoir, look out for a large boulder with cup and ring marks, at NZ 0330 9334. Not far from here there is a Bronze Age burial site, visible today as a mound of earth with a large stone slab in the centre. The walk continues west past Fallowlees Flush SSSI, a steep-sided valley, before heading back south across the moorland to Greenleighton Wood, and then back east to the top of Greenleighton Hill.

Wanney Byer

Two caves of 9m and 45m
Depths of 5m and 8m
Sandstone
Map: OL 42 – Kielder Water and Forest
NY 9336 8348
Moderate

Introduction
The Wanney Byer has been known about for centuries and probably gets its name from a belief that it was used as a den for wild animals. Byre is of course a word meaning cowshed, but it is hard to imagine cows gathering in this narrow rift. John Wallis described 'a remarkable fissure, or sinus, on the top of Great Waneyhouse Crag, called the Bier' in 1769, and John Hodgson, writing in 1820, said it was 'still frequented by foxes'. Whilst nowadays the moorland around the Wanney Crags is unpopulated by people, this has not always been the case. In a 1722 survey of Hawick and Sweethope, dwellings were recorded at the crags of both Great and Little Wanney with the names, 'Great Wannehouse' and 'Little Waney-house' respectively.

The byer is essentially a long, narrow fault that runs from west to east close to the edge of the crag and has boulders jammed in its roof for most of its length. It seems that these boulders were placed here to seal the rift and prevent animals from falling in. At various points underground, the rift is also partially or completely choked with boulders, hence there are separate caves here, rather than one continuous cave. Bear in mind that this is a deep chasm, which for much of its length is only separated from the surface world by jammed boulders, often hidden under dense heather, so do please be careful when wandering around at the top.

Various spellings have been used for this rift down the years, including Waney-byer, Wanny Byer, Waney Bier and Wanney Byre, so please feel free to call it by one of these other names in polite conversation.

Whilst this chasm had certainly been entered previously, and old editions of the *Northumberland Climbing Guide* refer to 'a quantity of subterranean climbing', in 1985 Peter Ryder and Richard Gibson of the Moldywarps

Speleological Group were the first to record details for the caving world. They surveyed Rift 1 and much of Rift 2, which they pushed eastwards as far as a boulder blockage. They also noted that there was a very narrow entrance further east. When I went to investigate, I found that this entrance beside a short vertical face of sandstone looked quite promising, so in January 2018 I returned with Carolina Smith de la Fuente of Black Rose Caving Club, Janet Kent of Durham Cave and Mine Club and David Keegan of the University of Newcastle Caving Club. We connected this narrow entrance with Rift 2 to increase the total length of recorded passage.

The route

Park at Fourlaws, near Sweethope Loughs, NY 943 829, and follow the footpath towards Great Wanney Crags. After 700m go through the gate and continue across the boggy open moor by a faint path, ignoring the path to the left, which follows the dry stone wall. A crossroads is reached on the ridge 300m from the wall. Go left here and walk close to the edge of the crag, following the

Chris Scaife at the entrance to Wanney Byer Rift 1   *Photo by Don Miller*

fissure that runs parallel to the crag. This fissure is the Wanney Byer and is visible on the surface for most of its length as a minor depression running in a straight line. At NY 9336 8348 the fissure meets the crag. At this point, on the face of the crag, there is a very short cave, blocked with boulders after a couple of metres. Rift 1 is a short distance east from the edge of the crag.

Wanney Byer Rift 1
Length 9m
Depth 5m
NY 9337 8348

This through trip is the ideal warm-up for the more strenuous Rift 2. Walk down into the obvious entrance, a narrow trench, and once underground, the slope continuing down soon chokes, but a scramble up leads to an entertaining exit squeeze.

Wanney Byer Rift 2
Length 45m
Depth 8m
NY 9339 8349

There are several entrances into this long section of the Wanney Byer. The widest is the 5m chimney that was used by the Moldywarps in 1985, and this entrance is about 30m to the east of the exit to Rift 1. There are a couple of large protruding boulders here and the entrance may be obscured by a large slab, but if this slab has been moved the way in will be revealed. This is a vertical drop without much in the way of handholds or footholds, so an electron ladder may be useful. The floor of the rift is soft soil and the walls are parallel and narrow for the entirety of the rift. The fragility of the ceiling is apparent when looking up from the floor, with lucid daylight glistering through in several places. From the foot of this climb/pitch, the rift can be followed westwards as far as the choke, beyond which is Rift 1.

In the opposite direction, the rift continues as far as a partial choke. There is a squeeze at the foot of a slope, followed by a tight squeeze downwards. This tight squeeze can be avoided by an awkward climb up towards daylight. It is possible to exit through Janet's Hole at the top of this climb, but there is more cave to be seen by continuing eastwards, first by a muddy crawl, then as a traverse over a chockstone. Below the traverse, the deepest part of the rift can be reached by descending to a ledge, then following the ledge back westwards a short distance, to a straightforward but narrow climb down. The rift then continues eastwards at a low level for a short distance, but it is very tight. Above, the traverse ends at another blockage, with an exit up an awkward climb and narrow squeeze. This emerges at NY 9342 8350, against a 1m vertical face in a section of exposed rock.

Svelte or ladderless cavers may find it more appealing to enter Rift 2 via this narrow entrance beside the vertical face, then traverse over the chockstone and descend below Janet's Hole to get into the long section of rift.

Make a day of it

In Northumberland and Tyneside, the phrase 'The Wilds of Wannie' is sometimes used to describe bleak and remote areas in general, and should give some idea as to the countryside here. This is excellent cycling country, with seemingly endless quiet roads through the moorland.

Great Wanney is a spectacular sandstone crag, offering some of the best rock climbing in the county. At the highest point of the crag, look for the semi-circular outline of an Iron Age hillfort.

The town of Bellingham is about 12km by road from the parking spot and is the starting point for a very pleasant walk. Hareshaw Linn is a picturesque waterfall and has its own car park in Bellingham, at NY 840 835. From here, there is a very obvious, well-marked path to the fall. Follow this for 2.5km and you will reach the vantage point for Hareshaw Linn. The western wall of this impressive sandstone gorge is undercut to make a long rock shelter, which reaches the dizzying length of 3.5m.

Shaftoe Hall

8m
Sandstone
Map: OL 42 – Kielder Water and Forest
NZ 0516 8165
Easy

Introduction
This is a small cave in a great location, with an interesting history.

James Radclyffe, the third Earl of Derwentwater, was one of Northumberland's key figures in the Jacobite Rising of 1715. When a government messenger pursued him for his role in the plot, he went into hiding and sought shelter in the fastnesses at Shaftoe Crags. He evaded capture at Shaftoe, but was taken prisoner after the Jacobite defeat at the Battle of Preston and, although many figures close to King George I petitioned for mercy, was executed at the Tower of London in 1716. It is said that Aurora Borealis showed so well on the night of his execution that for many years thereafter the Northern Lights were known colloquially as Lord Derwentwater's Lights. The Earls of Derwentwater took their names from the Cumbrian lake, but had their home at Dilston Castle, beside the Devil's Water near Corbridge.

The Punchbowl Stone, which sits atop the crag above the cave, is so named because a depression on the surface of the stone was enlarged in 1725 by Thomas Whittell, a capricious craftsman who, as a boy, had made his caprine arrival in nearby Cambo on the back of a goat. Having worked as a miller and a painter, Whittell moved on to stone masonry and whittled away at the rock to make a punchbowl that was filled with several gallons of intoxicating liquor for the wedding of Sir William Blackett, from nearby Wallington, to Lady Barbara Villiers, the daughter of the second Earl of Jersey. The pipers played from their chairs and the assembled guests danced drunkenly around a great bonfire, with Dionysian abandon.

The route
Follow the rough track west from Bolam West Houses, north-west of Bolam Lake, and park cars by the wall after the first cattle grid at NZ 063 823. From

here, follow the road on foot. This road bends left at a small lake, then right at East Shaftoe Hall Farm. After passing a row of cottages on the right a gate is reached, 1.2km from the parking place, which leads out onto the open moor, with woodland on the left-hand side. Stay on the main track for a further 400m, then head left towards the highest point of the ridge. The large boulder known as the Punchbowl Stone is a very distinctive feature just west of the highest point, and makes an excellent and quite popular viewpoint. The smaller boulder beside the Punchbowl Stone has had some adjustments made to it in the past to make a seat, and this is known as the Piper's Chair.

An oval Iron Age Hillfort, measuring 166m x 70m, sits on this site with the rocky crag forming a natural defence at its southern boundary. The multivallate lines of defence are clearly visible on the northern and eastern sides.

Shaftoe Hall is just below the Punchbowl Stone. The roomy rock shelter is fairly wide at the entrance and narrows towards the back; according to one 19th century guidebook writer, it could seat forty persons. Several extremely difficult bouldering problems have been put up in this cave by local climber

Chris Scaife in Shaftoe Hall   *Photo by Don Miller*

Bob Smith, with UK technical grades from 6b to 7a. There are also a few other very short caves nearby.

Make a day of it

The surrounding area, Shaftoe Crags, is probably the most extensive bouldering area in the county. The numerous boulders, buttresses and crags here offer climbing at all grades and anyone with an interest in bouldering (climbing without ropes to a relatively low height) will find that one day is not enough. The majority of the bouldering is to be found to the north of the cave, and on the scarp running east from the cave. The intricate features of Shaftoe Crags are worth exploring, even if you have no intention of bouldering. Mesolithic flints have been found in a rock shelter close to Salter's Nick Iron Age settlement, about 800m north of Shaftoe Hall. Another rock feature that is definitely worth seeing is The Tailor and his Man – a very large, split boulder close to the track below the crag, south-east of the cave.

If there is any time left in your day after exploring Shaftoe Crags, Bolam Lake Country Park is a very relaxing place to go for a short walk. As well as walking around the edge of the lake, there is some interesting woodland here.

The National Trust property and former home of punchbowl-loving Sir William Blackett, Wallington, is a short distance to the north-west of Shaftoe Crags. This is set in a large area of parkland, with lawns, ornamental lakes and woodland. More information can be found here:
https://www.nationaltrust.org.uk/wallington

Hartburn Grotto

6m
Sandstone
Map: OL42 – Kielder Water and Forest
NZ 0884 8654
Easy

Introduction
Situated in a small area of woodland known as Hartburn Glebe, this interesting sylvan grotto was carved out in about 1760 by Dr John Sharpe, the local vicar. There is some debate over whether this stately grotto is entirely man-made or if modifications were made to a natural cave, but it is certainly an interesting place worth visiting. Although it presumably had several uses, one was to provide changing facilities for women who bathed in the Hart Burn, which flows through this steep-sided glebe to its confluence with the River Wansbeck.

Postholes close to the grotto mark the location of the Roman bridge, believed to have been on the Devil's Causeway, that once crossed the Hart Burn here. The Devil's Causeway is a Roman road that stretches for roughly 89km (55 miles) from Dere Street just north of Corbridge, as far as Berwick-upon-Tweed, and although its actual route through Hartburn has been disputed down the years, this bridge is considered the most likely site of the river crossing. The proximity to the bridge has led some to speculate that Hartburn Grotto was used as an underground temple to the Roman god, Mithras.

The route
Park in the small lay-by at NZ 088 863, on the B6343 north-west of Hartburn Bridge, and take the steps down along the public footpath into Hartburn Glebe woodland. Follow this footpath down to the stream, where the path turns left, and after 300m you will reach the cave. There is a tall imposing entrance, with carved concavities above that once housed statues of Adam and Eve. This entrance leads into a heavily modified room with a fireplace on the right and Gothic archways to the left and straight ahead. The archway to the left is on a blank wall, but the archway straight ahead leads into a high, wide, short

Carolina Smith de la Fuente at the entrance

chamber at the back of the cave. A separate 7m tunnel, entirely man-made to preserve the modesty of the bathers, or to quote Dr Sharpe himself: 'for bathers along which they may pass unperceived by the impertinent eye of vulgar persons', leads from just outside the cave down to the Hart Burn.

Make a day of it
On exiting the cave, turn left to enjoy a pleasant circuit of this mature mixed woodland. The circuit of the glebe is roughly 1.1km long and includes some delightful views of the Hart Burn. In an article in *The Guardian* in 2011, Hartburn Glebe was voted one of the ten best British woods and forests for views.

Hartburn village itself is worth a visit. Dr John Sharpe, a busy man, also built the crenelated Tower House beside the glebe and modified the partly medieval Old Vicarage. The 11th century St Andrew's Church is worth a visit, particularly for its font from around 1250 and more recent but wonderfully decorated gravestones.

This is excellent cycling country, with numerous quiet minor roads and peaceful countryside. As the grotto is so easily reached from the road, and this cave can be explored without any specialist equipment – even a torch is something of a luxury in here – this cave is a worthy choice to visit as part of a day of cycling.

The historic county town of Northumberland, Morpeth, is 10km to the east of Hartburn and can be reached by following the B6343, which passes through the wonderful village of Mitford, with its Norman motte-and-bailey castle. Morpeth is a lively market town of great character, with several historic landmarks, including a 13th century chantry, a free-standing 17th century clock tower and the Georgian home of Admiral Lord Collingwood.

Alloa Lea Quarry Cave

10m
Five Yard Limestone in the Alston Block
Map: OL 43 – Hadrian's Wall, Haltwhistle and Hexham
NY 6837 6652
Easy

Introduction
This small cave is in a disused quarry close to Walltown Crags, a popular picnic spot on Hadrian's Wall. Any visitor to, or indeed resident of, Northumberland will surely be drawn to Hadrian's Wall, the great defensive fortification in Roman Britain, which ran from the River Tyne in the east to the Solway Firth in the west. The Wall is best preserved in this part of western Northumberland, with some sections close to Walltown still standing more than 1.5m high.

The nearby town of Haltwhistle lays claim to the title, 'Centre of Britain', being located at the mid-point of the longest north-south axis in the British Isles. Consequently, this cave is not simply at the heart of the county but at the heart of the country and whilst it may not lead to the centre of the Earth, it is the underground gateway of choice for those looking to Journey to the Centre of Britain.

This cave was first identified by John Grundy in 1987 and then explored by Peter Ryder, of the Moldywarps Speleological Group, with his four-year-old son, Aidan. The very tight squeeze on the right was dug out at this time and the littlun got through into the tiny chamber beyond.

This is a small cave that can undoubtedly add interest to any visit to this fascinating area.

The route
Follow the small road heading east, opposite the Roman Army Museum just off the B6318 near Greenhead. After 800m there is a car parking spot on the left, NY 675 662, marked 'Walltown Crags'. Please park here, as the road beyond is intended for farm traffic only. Walk along the road for 1km to a large lime kiln on the left. This lime kiln has been made from stones taken from Hadrian's Wall, as in fact have most stone-built structures in the area.

Chris Scaife in the very tight squeeze   *Photo by Don Miller*

Alloa Lea Quarry is just uphill behind the lime kiln and the cave is the obvious hole in the centre of the quarry face.

The passage soon lowers to a flat-out junction. On the right is a very tight squeeze, for small cavers only, which leads into a small phreatic chamber with flowstone walls and impassable exit rifts. Left from the junction is a rising squeeze into a chamber. A small tube running off from here (too tight to enter) leads to a speck of daylight coming in from a small hole in the hillside above the rock face.

Make a day of it

For a wonderful circuit of the local area, return to the small road in front of the Alloa Lea Quarry and turn left. Follow the road a short distance and where left leads up to Alloa Lea Farm, continue straight ahead on the unsurfaced byway, which heads south-east to the Vallum. The Vallum is a huge earthwork that runs to the south of Hadrian's Wall for practically its entire length. The byway follows the course of the Vallum east for about 1km and then joins a tarmacked road coming from Cockmount Farm. Continue east on the now-tarmacked road for a further 600m to a junction. The farm track uphill to the left leads, after 300m, to the south-east corner of Aesica, or Great Chesters, Roman Fort. Aesica was one of the major forts on Hadrian's Wall and its perimeter wall is well preserved, although there is not much left of the interior. Farm buildings, built over the route of the Wall, now occupy the north-east corner of the fort.

From the fort, follow Hadrian's Wall Path, which in this area is also the Pennine Way, for a very scenic 3.3km walk to Walltown Crags. The Wall is well preserved here, with several turrets, and in parts the natural crags of the Whin Sill have been incorporated into the Wall. A short distance past Walltown Crags is Turret 45A. This watch tower is believed to have been built prior to the Wall itself, probably associated with the Roman Road Stanegate, which linked Coria (Corbridge) in the east with Luguvalium (Carlisle) in the west.

Immediately west of Turret 45A is one of the best-preserved sections of the entire Wall, reaching heights over 1.5m. To visit the Roman Army Museum, follow Hadrian's Wall Path for a further 800m, then turn left and walk about 100m along the minor road. From the Army Museum, follow the road east for 800m to return to the car parking spot. For more information about the museum, see **www.vindolanda.com/roman-army-museum**

BELLCRAG CAVE

45m
Limestone
Map: OL 43 – Hadrian's Wall, Haltwhistle and Hexham
NY 7728 7200
Moderate

Introduction
This limestone cave is found in the sylvan surroundings of Wark Forest at the southern end of Kielder Forest, the largest area of woodland in England. There is shallow limestone over quite a large part of this region, and several karstic features, such as shakeholes and underground streams; but to date this is the only significant cave recorded.

Bellcrag Cave, with its obvious entrance where a stream disappears right beside the forestry track, has been known about for years and was previously measured as just 8m long, at which point the passage was blocked with flood debris. When I visited in 2014, with Don Miller of Black Rose Caving Club, we found that this obstruction was no longer present, and that the streamway continued, so I returned the following year with Carolina Smith de la Fuente, also of Black Rose. On the 4th of July 2015 we stayed at the excellent nearby Haughtongreen Bothy and used a shovel, borrowed from the bothy, to dig around a silt blockage to the left of a tiny hole, into which the stream disappeared after 26m. After celebrating the independence of the route from the streamway for a short distance, we pushed the cave to its present length of 45m, making it the longest cave in Northumberland National Park. It does have the rather magical quality of being a passage north of Hadrian's Wall heading south, which may conjure up images of a natural secret passage underneath the Wall. Unfortunately, the current limit is some way short of this mythical connection.

Please note that the streamway beyond the first 8m is very muddy, so a full set of caving clothing is advised. The cave fills to the roof when the stream is in spate, so this is a cave best left for drier weather conditions.

The route
The most interesting approach to Bellcrag Cave is to park at NY 794 684 at the Vercovicium Roman Fort, also known as Housesteads. This is a

dramatically situated Roman fort, currently in the care of English Heritage and open daily. Check the English Heritage website for current prices and more information prior to visiting: http://www.english-heritage.org.uk/visit/places/housesteads-roman-fort-hadrians-wall/

After visiting the fort, head left along Hadrian's Wall for 1km, passing Housesteads Crags and Cuddy's Crags, then head right along the Pennine Way. Alternatively, if not visiting the Roman fort, park at a small lay-by at NY 783 679, on the B6318 west of Housesteads Roman Fort. Follow the path north for 700m to Hadrian's Wall, then join the Pennine Way. Heading north, pass between Greenlee Lough and Broomlee Lough and after just over 2km, reach the edge of the forest at NY 780 707. (The first path off to the right, 200m into the forest, leads, after 800m, to Haughtongreen Bothy. If planning an overnight stay in the area, this bothy is highly recommended, particularly in the summer months when camping is ill-advised owing to the active midge population.)

Continue on the main track through the forest. About 1km after the turn off for the bothy, the Pennine Way separates from the main track. Stay on the main track for a further 600m, then an obvious track turns left. After about 400m take the grassy track right, then after another 300m take the grassy track left. Continue 300m farther down this path and a stream can be seen on the right-hand side, disappearing into the small entrance to Bellcrag Cave.

The stream entering Bellcrag Cave in winter

Clamber down into the wide entrance chamber, which contains a few small speleothems – a rare sight this far north. After 8m the Haughtongreen Passage is reached, and the way on becomes a crawl in the winding stream, with the walls and ceiling caked in mud. At 26m from the entrance the stream passes through a very small hole, which can be bypassed by a muddy crawl to the left. This is where the silt blockage was dug out in 2015. Beyond this the cave continues as a tortuous muddy streamway, diminishing in size, until 45m from the outside world the ceiling gets too low for further progress. The final few metres are quite testing, with mud everywhere and a stream that may rise around a human body blocking much of the passage. It is best not to linger in this section, and be aware that the only turning space is behind you, so you will need to reverse a short distance before turning around.

Make a day of it

Bellcrag Cave is situated near the UNESCO World Heritage Site of Hadrian's Wall and within Kielder Forest, close to both the Pennine Way and Hadrian's Wall Path, so there are numerous opportunities to extend your day, or even longer. Returning to the main track through the forest at NY 778 724 and turning left leads, after 300m, to the Bellcrag Flow nature reserve, a wildlife-rich part of the Border Mires, particularly good for peat specialist species such as the large heath butterfly.

The nearby Roman Wall Loughs – Greenlee Lough, Broomlee Lough and Crag Lough – are naturally occurring eutrophic lakes and are internationally important wetland sites, with unusual aquatic plantlife including several species of very pollution-sensitive pondweed and stonewort. Lough, pronounced loff, is a local word meaning lake. As well as plants, the loughs are good for butterflies, dragonflies and birds. Greenlee Lough is the easiest lough to visit in combination with Bellcrag Cave and can be reached by following the track to the west from the edge of the forest at NY 780 707. This track continues for just over 1km past the farms East and West Stonefolds and then to a ford. Just after the ford a path through the hay meadow leads to the bird hide at NY 769 700. The meadow here is at its best in late June or early July and a short distance past the bird hide is a 500m boardwalk through the reed beds.

Queen's Cave

8m
Sandstone
Map: OL 43 – Hadrian's Wall
NY 9041 6160
Easy

Introduction
This cave is found in West Dipton Wood, which is a fascinating, long, narrow stretch of woodland around West Dipton Burn just south of Hexham. The walk to the cave involves crossing a fairly large stream several times and is best done in wellies.

The cave gets its name because, according to local legend, Queen Margaret of Anjou (the wife of Henry VI) and her son, Prince Edward, hid in this cave following the Lancastrians' defeat in the Battle of Hexham in 1464, during the War of the Roses. A 'robber, of gigantic stature', with his sword drawn, approached Queen Margaret and her son after the battle, but on being instructed by the queen to save the son of the king, he led them to the cave. They remained hidden there for two days.

The route
There is ample parking at NY 930 610 opposite the Dipton Mill Inn, a cosy pub with good real ales, on the Dipton Mill Road south of Hexham. Walk north up the road for 50m, across the road bridge, then turn left into the woodland, signposted 'Public Footpath. West Dipton Wood'. Follow this path through the mostly deciduous steep-sided woodland, which is very pretty and varied. There are several paths in this part of the wood, but they all unite, so just keep heading west and after 1.5km you will reach a footbridge.

Stay on the north bank but keep close to the burn. After 300m you will reach a small crag on the north bank where it is necessary to cross the stream. From this point to the cave West Dipton Burn must be crossed several times. Rather than describe each crossing point I will leave it up to you to decide the most enjoyable route. Blackburn Crag is soon passed on the south bank, and Black Burn flows into West Dipton Burn from the south. About 700m upstream of

Chris Scaife in the entrance   *Photo by Don Miller*

the confluence with Black Burn, having passed several interesting crags and rocky buttresses, a small stream cascades down the north side of the wood and just beyond this you will see a large crag on the south bank. Queen's Cave is located at the foot of the westernmost unbroken part of this crag.

The small entrance leads into a cave 8m long and 7m wide. The walls are of very crumbly, soft sandstone and the floor is muddy with a hint of rubble. There is a flat ceiling, never more than 1.5m high, so presumably most of Queen Margaret's time in hiding was spent crouching. Or perhaps she had already fled to France by the time of the Battle of Hexham and didn't hide in this cave at all.

Make a day of it

The footpath through West Dipton Wood continues west for a further 1.5km, passing Cat Crags and a couple of waterfalls. At the westernmost end there is a footbridge and then a steep path out of the gorge. This path stays just north of the wood and passes through farmland, then returns into the wood and heads towards the footbridge over the burn. Staying north of the burn, it is now 1.5km back to the Dipton Mill Inn.

Hexham is a delightful market town to the north. Amongst the many historical buildings in the town centre are a 15th century gatehouse known as the Moot Hall, and one of the first purpose-built jails in England, now home to the Old Gaol museum. Hexham Abbey is a fantastic example of Early English Gothic architecture, on a site that has had a church since the year 674. The Anglo Saxon crypt still remains and is open to visitors. See the Hexham Abbey website for more information: **https://www.hexham-abbey.org.uk**

The North Pennines Area of Outstanding Natural Beauty

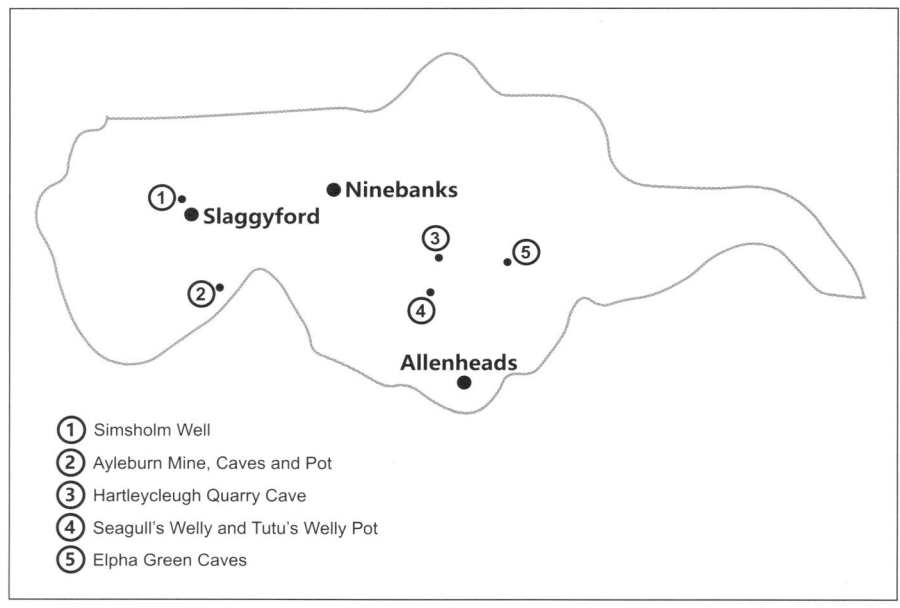

Cave locations in the North Pennines AONB

The south-west of Northumberland sits at the northern tip of the North Pennines Area of Outstanding Natural Beauty. This area is known for its remote moorland but thanks to its mineral-rich geology it also has a substantial industrial heritage and there are many disused mines and quarries. The wildlife is also noteworthy in this area, with significant populations of otter, red squirrel, black grouse and ring ouzel.

Anyone keen to explore the area on foot should consider the 58km (36 mile) Isaac's Tea Trail walk, a waymarked circuit that passes through Ninebanks, Allendale, Nenthead and Alston and goes quite close to all of the caves in this section. The walk is named after Isaac Holden, a lead miner who became a door-to-door tea salesman following the closure of the Mohope lead mines.

The official start of the walk is in Allendale Town at Isaac's Well, NY 838 558, a source of clean drinking water constructed thanks to funds raised by Isaac Holden, which according to the plaque, 'not only helped overcome the threat of cholera and typhoid but also made better tasting tea.'

The limestone in this southern part of Northumberland is far more extensive than anywhere else in the county, so the caves here are of a different character, one more in keeping with the classic limestone caves of the Northern Dales. Whereas many caves elsewhere in this guide are perfectly suited to a visit wearing walking clothing and armed only with a torch, all of the caves in this section are best tackled with full caving gear, including undersuit, oversuit, wellies, kneepads and a helmet.

Northumberland's Pennine caves are found in valleys formed by tributaries of the Tyne. There is much limestone in South Tynedale and the area near Alston, which lends its name to the Alston Block of the Great Limestone. Whilst Alston itself is just across the border in Cumbria, some of the finest caves in the vicinity of Alston are located in Northumberland. East of Tynedale are West Allen Dale and East Allen Dale. The River West Allen reaches a confluence with the East Allen at the wonderfully named Water Meetings, in an idyllic spot near Cupola Bridge on the A686, to form the River Allen. This

Moorland between East and West Allen Dale

river then flows into the South Tyne near Bardon Mill. The limestone is exposed in only a small part of the Allen Dales and there is much boulder clay on the surface, so very few limestone outcrops. There are, however, several excellent caves.

There are two caves in this part of the county that are listed in *Northern Caves* but are currently inaccessible. The mined entrance to Ayleburn Mine Cave is currently blocked, although this situation may change and it is possible that in the future a connection will be made from Ayleburn Caves or Pot. A pothole of 9m depth, called Windy Hall Pot, was previously recorded beside the Ayle to Barhaugh road at NY 700 505. Following an extensive search of the nearby area, it appears that this hole has now been filled in.

Simsholm Well

6m
Limestone
Map: OL43 – Hadrian's Wall
NY 6718 5277
Moderate

Introduction
Simsholm Well is a small cave in Knarsdale in the South Tyne valley. This is in quite a large area of limestone that must surely be harbouring more caves. There are several nearby springs, or resurgences, marked on the Ordnance Survey map and bearing the name, 'Well'. Unfortunately, most of these are tiny springs of little speleological interest. The only cave currently known, Simsholm Well, is located very close to the Knar Burn, which is the destination of the small stream flowing out of the entrance.

Simsholm Well was first explored by the Moldywarps Speleological Group in the summer of 1985. They very sensibly lowered the water level of the resurgence pool before entering. This exposed a damp, tubular crawl. In the absence of caving gear, Richard Gibson apparently stripped off and entered the tube in 'a state of nature', while others sat on the sidelines shouting their encouragement. On the same day the Moldywarps had a look at Ash Well, at NY 670 531, which is currently choked with large limestone blocks, but could potentially reward determined diggers.

The railway viaduct, built in 1852 for the Alston Line that linked Alston with Haltwhistle on the Newcastle-Carlisle railway, is a very imposing structure that will be passed en route. The standard gauge branch line between Alston and Haltwhistle was closed in 1976, but thanks to the voluntary work of the South Tynedale Railway Preservation Society there is now a narrow-gauge heritage line in operation, known as the South Tynedale Railway.

The route
Park near Slaggyford Methodist Church at NY 677 524, just uphill from the A689. Follow the Pennine Way north for 600m to a footbridge over the Knar Burn. The impressive railway viaduct is on the left. Cross the bridge, then head

left, leave the path and follow the north bank of the burn. Head upstream until a large, flat grassy area is on the opposite (south) side of the burn. Cross the burn wherever you can at this point. The smaller stream entering the Knar Burn on the south bank here emanates from Simsholm Well.

This resurgence is a constricted, tubular crawl in deep water and may require some excavation. After a short distance, the cave comes to an abrupt end with a collapsed roof. Some tree roots, and indeed some knars, are present in the collapse.

Make a day of it

This is a very pleasant area for walking and cycling, with a number of footpaths and bridleways. The Pennine Way and Pennine Cycleway can both be followed from Slaggyford in either direction. Following the Pennine Way south from Slaggyford for 4.3km will take you along the South Tyne valley, past Kirkhaugh station, to Whitley Castle Roman Fort (NY 695 486). This unusually-shaped fort, known to the Romans as Epiacum, is said to have the most complex defensive earthworks of any known fort in the entire Roman Empire. It was built in the early 2nd century, at about the same time as Hadrian's Wall. As well as providing support for the defence of Hadrian's Wall, the fort seems to have been associated with the control of lead mines in the area. Epiacum is currently open access, year-round. Not far from the fort, at NY 6920 4878, the Lort Burn emanates from the hillside at Epiacum Resurgence. The low, wet entrance looks fairly promising, but this cavelet is choked after just 4m.

Railway viaduct across the Knar Burn

For a short circuit of Knars Dale, head from Simsholm Well back to the viaduct and follow the footpath going south-west, on the north bank of the burn. The path briefly follows the edge of the field, then returns to the woodland over a stile. The path is not always very clear but stay low down and close to the burn until NY 662 518, where a bridleway is taken on the left down to a footbridge across the Knar Burn. Follow the path on the south side of the burn as far as Greenhaugh Farm, where a footpath heading slightly uphill to the right leads back to Slaggyford. This area is particularly good for wildlife, such as pied flycatcher, red squirrel and roe deer.

For a more sedate extension to your day, the South Tynedale Railway is an obvious choice. Steam locomotives operate four times daily along the short route on most days between March and October. For more information about this railway, take a look at the website: **http://www.south-tynedale-railway.org.uk**

Ayleburn Mine Cave

Length 1,700m
Depth 30m
Great Limestone
Map: OL 31 – North Pennines
NY 7276 4977
Difficult
Entrance currently blocked

Introduction

Ayleburn Mine Cave is the longest cave in Northumberland by a country mile, but lamentably, the entrance is currently sealed and access is not possible. It is included in this book for completeness and in the sanguine hope that cavers will one day be allowed to return to explore its depths.

The Ayle Burn is a tributary of the South Tyne, which it joins north of the joint highest market town in England, Alston. Although Alston itself is in Cumbria, the Ayle Burn forms the boundary with Northumberland, so the caves with entrances on the north bank of the burn – Ayleburn Mine Cave, Ayleburn Caves and Ayleburn Pot – are in Northumberland.

By far the largest of these, and the first to have been explored, is the 1.7km Ayleburn Mine Cave. The mine level was driven by the London Lead Company in the late 18th century, at the dawn of an era of intense lead-mining in the local area. The miners found approximately 200m of natural cave, but no lead; so their mine became a show cave, with visitors hauled up a shaft in a basket and then shown the streamway by candlelight. At some point in the 19th century it was apparently forgotten about and effectively lost.

The cave was re-discovered by a team from Cambridge University Caving Club, led by Brian Heys, in 1948. This team produced a survey of about 200m of cave passage, downstream from the mine level. This was effectively the old cave, as explored long before, and ended in a low, wet bedding plane. Later, further exploration was carried out by Durham Cave Club, who passed a waterfall just upstream of the mine passage, and explored about another 200m, ending in a wet crawl where the ceiling gets too low.

The Moldywarps Speleological Group first visited in April 1969, having heard a story that miners had put chaff into the cave's stream and had observed it emerging from a spring called Saffron Well, over two miles to the north at NY 6925 5145. Nowadays fluorescent dyes, such as fluorescein, are normally used for tracing the flow of underground water – as well as for making the Chicago River green for St Patrick's Day – but back then subterraneous hydrologists used chaff, feathers or tagged eels.

Over the course of several trips that year, Moldywarps cavers including Colin Carson, Leslie Beevers and Stuart Hodgson, as well as Alan and Dave Brook from the University of Leeds Speleological Association, managed to pass the low section that had been the downstream limit in 1948, and explored the cave as far as a large chamber, which was named Rumney Cavern after a workman who had been killed by a massive falling rock in the very early days of the mine. The tight squeeze that led into the Moldywarps' extensions was first passed by Colin Carson, whose wetsuit was left in shreds, hanging around his waist. It is hence known as the Banana Peeler.

Upstream extensions in Gutgrinder Inlet were made between 1975 and 1973, by Moldywarps cavers Peter Ryder, Stuart Hodgson, Kev Solman, John Dale, Chris Langthorne and Dave and Keith Errington. Much persistence was needed to push some tortuous, narrow passage known as The Contortions, which eventually led into easier passage, with a stalactite grille blockage after about 100m. This was later passed, without much harm to the stalactites, and a short crawl was followed, which soon became too low for further progress. An easy crawl, Coward's Entry, was also found, which made it possible to access the end of Gutgrinder Inlet without twisting and turning through The Contortions.

Cave diver Jerry Murland, hoping to make an appearance at Saffron Well, explored downstream in 1975 and got as far as a third sump. In 1992, cave divers Jon Watt, Malcolm Bass and Paul Monico from the University of Leeds Speleological Association, made a few trips to the downstream sumps, during which time they measured them accurately and explored the complex third sump. Being more modern types than the miners of the past, they decided to try dye tracing and found that the chaff test story had been an empty husk; the water emanated at Alders Gill, NY 7195 4940, just a few hundred metres due south, on the north bank of the Ayle Burn. Whether the result of mendacious miners or falsified folklore, the specious account of the chaff testing had nonetheless spurred on the exploration of Northumberland's longest cave.

The route
The natural cave passage begins 9m above a Y-junction in the mine level. The rise was usually tackled by sending up the best climber first, who would use some solid, wedged beams for a belay, and lower a ladder for the rest of the group. A short scramble down to the left then leads into the stream passage.

Upstream, after 15m, is the free-climbable waterfall that was the limit of exploration before Durham Cave Club pushed through the boulder choke and squeeze above, into the upstream passage. Gutgrinder Inlet is on the right and begins with a tight crawl, The Contortions, for about 50m, to a chamber, where the 10m Coward's Entry can be used to rejoin the main streamway. Gutgrinder Inlet continues, easier going for about another 60m until it becomes too low.

The main passage continues upstream from above the waterfall for about 200m, first as easy walking, then to stooping height. A sandy oxbow provides a bypass to a long duck and leads back to the stream, in a low, wide bedding. Far Upstream Passage is a wet crawl, with formations, becoming too low just a few metres from the stream in Ayleburn Pot.

The Downstream Series begins with a 3m climb into a dry passage. Straight ahead is Upper Grotesque Passage, which is mostly narrow crawling – and has this name because the 19th century visitors thought that the rock formations looked like petrified aquiline and vulpine heads – but right leads back to the stream. The stream passage lowers to a crawl, then flows into an impassably tight bedding. The way on is through a dry tube. After a small chamber, the First Squeeze, also known as the Banana Peeler, is reached – an elliptic tube

Colin Carson in the Banana Peeler   *Photo by Peter Ryder*

20cm high and 40cm wide. Neoprene will inevitably be peeled away from your upper body here in a musaceous manner.

The stream is soon rejoined and the passage continues as a mixture of crawling and stooping to the Second Squeeze, formed by a boulder in the passage, easier than the first. Down several cascades in a wide, boulder-strewn passage, leads into vadose streamway, which becomes walking height. Just above the stream, on the left, is the 20m sandy-floored High Level Oxbow, and 10m downstream from this is a series of interconnecting sandy crawls known as Lombardy. The streamway continues through a sharp double bend with a pool of water that looks sufficiently sump-like to have fooled the original explorer and is therefore known as Stuart's Folly. After some more walking passage there is a 46m inlet passage on the left, but the main stream heads to a small waterfall, which lowers into Rumney Cavern. This chamber is 15m long, 6m wide and up to 6m high.

A short crawl from Rumney Cavern leads to the 4m, constricted, Sump 1. Although short, it is quite tricky, so free-diving should not be attempted. The muddy, 12m Sump 2 is reached after 17m of muddy canal. Sump 3 follows shortly afterwards and begins as a steep slope to a depth of 4m, then a wide passage continues for 10m to an airspace. Following the results of the dye tracing, which debunked the theory that the cave would continue to Saffron Well, and as it appeared unlikely that more dry passage would be found, the cave has not been dived beyond this airspace.

Make a day of it

If you are lucky enough to live in a better world, one fine day when this entrance is unsealed, and have completed the trips in this cave as well as the adjacent Ayleburn Caves and Ayleburn Pot, then I suggest a trip to the pub to celebrate.

Ayleburn Caves 1 and 2 (now connected)

96m total
Great Limestone
Map: OL 31 – North Pennines
NY 7297 4990 (Cave 1) and NY 7299 4992 (Cave 2)
Moderate

Introduction
During the Moldywarps Speleological Group's many trips to explore and survey Ayleburn Mine Cave in 1969 and 1970, the Ayleburn Caves and Pot were also surveyed for the first time, having undoubtedly been previously entered but not recorded. These caves are part of the same system as the mine cave, but do not currently have passable connections with it. They are, however, very enjoyable caves in their own right and well worth a visit. The typical Northern Dales limestone character is evident here, with sharp-sided rifts and numerous small side passages.

When the two Ayleburn Caves were initially surveyed, by Moldywarps members Peter Ryder, John Cooper, Lesley Worth and Colin Carson, there was a connecting passage between the two, which was blocked with 'rather fine formations'. Regrettably, in recent years these ethereal formations have been destroyed and removed by vandals, meaning that a through trip is now possible. The connection is quite narrow, so some people may still prefer to treat them as two separate caves.

The Ayleburn Caves are situated on land that currently belongs to Shepherds Solid Fuel. Prior to any visit, permission to cross their land should be sought by phoning the company on 01434 381158.

The route
If permission has been given by the owners of the quarry, the caves can be accessed by crossing the private land owned by Shepherds Solid Fuel, which is situated at NY 728 498, beside the Ayle Burn on the minor road between Ayle and Clarghyll. There are several cave entrances on the north bank of the burn just past the quarry: some very small caves as well as Ayleburn Caves 1 and 2, and the new entrance to Ayleburn Pot. The entrance to Cave 1 is the big, square entrance nearest to the quarry.

The entrance to Ayleburn Cave 1

Crawl into the passage going straight into the hillside. This soon enlarges to standing height and can be followed, through some large boulders, to a blank-walled aven. A few metres back from the aven, on the right-hand side when going in, is a 2m crawl leading into the rest of the cave. A little closer to the entrance from this crawl, a metre or so off the ground, is a very tight rift connection into the same chamber, through sharp rock, which should only be attempted by those who value neither their oversuits nor their skin.

Once through the crawl, which emerges in a boulder-filled chamber, the way on is to the left. Crawl through the obvious passage, which has a standing-height blind rift running parallel to it, into a crawl that goes around a corner and enlarges enough to turn around just before becoming too tight. About half way along this crawl, a narrow passage to the right is the connection with Ayleburn Cave 2. The formations are all gone now, so there is no moral reason not to do the through trip, although it is quite narrow so there may be certain physical barriers. Anyone unable to fit through this passage that now connects Caves 1 and 2 can reverse Cave 1 from here, then enter Cave 2 through the rectangular hole at the foot of the scar, at NY 7299 4992.

Once through the narrow connection, there is a T-junction with a rift. To the left soon becomes too tight, but to the right continues to a blockage. There are some jammed rocks in the rift above at this point and it is possible to free-climb up either before or after these rocks, then thrutch along and downwards into the continuation of the rift, which soon reaches another, perpendicular rift.

At this crossroads, straight ahead soon chokes and to the right is a too-tight connection with Cave 1. The 6m of passage to the left from the crossroads is of Brobdingnagian proportions for this part of the world, and ends at a deep pit, which can be descended by climbing down the right-hand wall. From the bottom of this pit the ceiling is 8m above. Climbing out of the pit, you will see that the ceiling ahead is very flat, the floor anything but. Continue forwards and slide out through Ayleburn Cave 2 entrance, which is the rectangular hole at the foot of the scar. This is 25m upstream from Cave 1, at NY 7299 4992.

Make a day of it

Ayleburn Pot is only a few metres away, so can easily be visited on the same day. The market town of Alston, just 5km away, is known for its charming cobbled streets, particularly the steep main street, which has a characterful market cross. Many of the stone buildings in Alston date from the 17th century. There are also plenty of shops, cafes and pubs if possessions, food and alcohol is what you're after. Anyone looking to stay overnight will be pleased to learn that Alston has an excellent Youth Hostel. The last time I stayed in this hostel, I spent my entire breakfast time watching red squirrels through the window.

Ayleburn Pot

Length 223m
Depth 12m
Great Limestone
Map: OL 31 – North Pennines
NY 7300 4993
Moderate/Difficult

Introduction

Ayleburn Pot was first recorded by the Moldywarps Speleological Group in 1970, having been visited in conjunction with Ayleburn Mine Cave when the mine cave was being explored and surveyed. At this time the pot was pushed to just 20m long and 10m deep. Having used what is now, in these enlightened times, known as the Old Entrance, Dave and Keith Errington reached the stream, but found that the stream passage was choked in both directions after a short distance.

Significant extensions were made by Chris Fuller and Steve Torran of Oxford University Cave Club and the University of Leeds Speleological Association in 1977. Steve Torran had taken a friend, David Botton from Rothbury, to Ayleburn Mine Cave as an introduction to caving. Whilst David relaxed in the sun after turning back at the Banana Peeler, as was the wont of many cavers in there, Steve – who had continued solo to the sump in Ayleburn Mine Cave – had a quick poke into Ayleburn Pot. He was expecting it to be a very short trip, but found a dry side passage leading away from the stream, which had seemingly been overlooked in the past, and he broke into the unknown. He returned several times over the next few months with Chris Fuller, to explore and survey this impressive cave.

Shortly afterwards, the Errington brothers of the Moldywarps returned and opened up the New Entrance to the pot, which is currently the only way in as the Old Entrance is clogged with waste. At some point since then, there has been the addition of a 20m rift, reached through a U-bend squeeze, near the upstream end and the Old Entrance. This must have been the result of a dig, but does not seem to have been recorded anywhere, so I am sadly unable to credit the plucky explorers here.

This is quite a hard trip with significant loose rock and several narrow squeezes. It should only be undertaken by experienced cavers.

This pot is situated on land that currently belongs to Shepherds Solid Fuel. Prior to any visit, permission to cross their land should be sought by phoning the company on 01434 381158.

The route

Approach as for Ayleburn Caves, which you may remember as: If permission has been given by the owners of the quarry, the caves can be accessed by crossing the private land owned by Shepherds Solid Fuel, which is situated at NY 728 498, beside the Ayle Burn on the minor road between Ayle and Clarghyll. The New Entrance to Ayleburn Pot is the last cave you will see between the quarry and the large fence upstream, at the lowest point of the last exposed section of limestone. The Old Entrance, in a shallow open pot, is just up the hill from here, but is currently blocked with all manner of farm rubbish after a short distance.

Slide down into a small chamber, then either go straight ahead in a fairly constricted crawl, or left then right to get to the same point, again fairly constricted. Continue to Holes Junction. Right from here leads into a crawl, which goes around a right-hand bend, then descends to a T-Junction. Going right at this junction, through a U-bend squeeze, leads into a standing-height 20m rift, which ends at a boulder choke with some delicate formations. Left

The New Entrance

from the T-Junction, squeeze through some sharp rock to get into the stream. This streamway is currently blocked in both directions, but with much excavation of the gravelly stream bed, a determined digger may be able to continue upstream in a low-airspace wet crawl, then follow a short crawl in dry passage on the right into an ascending rift, before being confronted with the farm rubbish just inside the Old Entrance.

Left from Holes Junction goes into a passage that soon leads to a 2m drop down into the streamway. The stream can be followed along a low-airspace crawl to a sump, which is very close to the upstream end of Ayleburn Mine Cave. Continuing in the dry passage above the 2m drop is a crawl around a couple of bends, which soon enlarges into a complex breakdown passage. At the far end of this passage, there is a way through the jumble of rocks on the right into a lower passage with iron-stained formations. Heading up this passage there are two small passages on the left. The first is too tight, but the second leads into a sizeable rift. There is a high aven on the right, which can be climbed with care, and a very short section of streamway can also be entered from this rift; but to get to the farthest extremity in the cave, follow the rift by the left-hand wall. A narrow and slightly tricky climb up enters a final tall aven.

Make a day of it
In addition to visiting the nearby Ayleburn Caves and Alston, walking opportunities are plentiful in the surrounding countryside. Apart from Alston, the nearest town of any size is about 30km away, and to the west lies a great expanse of remote moorland that will appeal to all those who enjoy vast open spaces.

Hartlecleugh Quarry Cave

383m
Great Limestone
Map: OL 31 – North Pennines
NY 8041 4864
Difficult

Introduction

Hartleycleugh Quarry Cave is the longest known cave in West Allen Dale and, whilst the entrance to Ayleburn Mine Cave remains blocked, the longest accessible cave in Northumberland.

Although this cave was apparently well known locally, and used fairly frequently by an outdoor activity centre, for many years, it was not known to the caving world until 1987, and has never appeared in any caving guidebooks. Exploration of the sections of the cave beyond that visited by locals and the outdoor activity centre was apparently undertaken concurrently over numerous trips by members and friends of the Moldywarps Speleological Group (Peter and Elaine Ryder, Peter Bradley and Tim Elliot) and the Haymarket Caving Club (Jimmy Roy, John Dobinson and Peter Eagan), each club unaware of the other's stealthy visits until one evening they bumped into each other at the entrance.

Please note: there are two other quarries marked within the same grid square on the Ordnance Survey map. The cave is not at either of these, but in another quarry, which is not marked on the map.

This cave contains an active streamway, which rises quickly and some sections will fill to the roof, so it should only be entered during dry, settled weather. The entrance is on private land and permission should be obtained from the landowner at Greenleycleugh Farm prior to visiting the cave.

The route

This hidden cave is very close to the road that runs from Hartleycleugh on the West Allen Dale Road, north-west through Limestone Brae and Ninebanks, then joins the A686 just near Carr's Burn. There is no particularly good place to park on this road; it is best to park beside the track at the junction from the West Allen Dale Road, at NY 806 485.

Directly opposite the house known as Low Hartley Cleugh, which is 400m along the road, there is a metal gate, leading onto a grassy, overgrown track that heads down to the stream, known as Hartley Cleugh. Follow this track south-east, upstream, and soon you will have a fence on your right-hand side, beside the Hartley Cleugh, and the quarry wall on the left-hand side. Shortly after the fence on the right-hand side and quarry wall on the left-hand side come to an end, a dry stream bed crosses the track. Scramble up the dried-out waterfall here to get to the tall, narrow entrance.

Just inside the entrance is a short section of narrow, walking-height passage, but most of the first 45m is crawling and scrambling over boulders along Boot-Trapper Passage. This leads to a T-junction with the streamway. Left from here, downstream, is narrow and awkward, becoming too tight after about 70m. Upstream, right, from the T-junction is a wet crawl, the First Wallow, leading to a squeeze over boulders into Claydome Chamber. This is an unusual chamber roofed by boulder clay, seemingly without any limestone above.

A long, low-airspace duck, known as Quaaack, is the way on upstream. This begins as a constricted, wet crawl and ends with a very low ceiling on the left to get into larger passage beyond. There should be just enough airspace here to avoid a free-dive. The streamway beyond is much easier, with stooping initially,

Boot-Trapper Passage

then a 30m straight crawl to Elaine's Squeeze. Thrutching through this squeeze leads into a chamber with a precarious boulder dangling above. This squeeze and sword of Damocles can be avoided by the Haymarket Flyover, a narrow crawl reached by climbing up just before Elaine's Squeeze, which drops into the passage just past the chamber. Beyond this point, the cave changes its dimensions and becomes walking passage with some pretty formations. A crawl down a short side passage to the right, not long after the Haymarket Flyover, leads to a blind 2m shaft that, curiously, drops lower than the stream passage.

Back on the main passage, the rising floor soon necessitates hands and knees crawling, followed by a sudden drop in the ceiling towards Sump One. This 6m long, shallow dive through a low and muddy bedding plane has been dived by cave diver Mike Thomas, who found 9m of dry passage beyond, followed by the rather blue Sump Two, which has not yet been dived. Those picturing beautiful cerulean waters may be disheartened to learn that this hue is the result of pollutants. Perhaps nowhere is untouched by mankind's devastation of the natural world.

Make a day of it

Most cavers will wish to combine a visit to this cave with its near neighbours, Seagull's Welly Pot and Tutu's Welly Pot, which are just a short drive away. Hartleycleugh Quarry Cave is by far the wettest of these three though, so should probably be the last one you visit if that is your itinerary. Anyone visiting all three of these caves is unlikely to be looking for any lengthy ventures to add to their day out, but the remote countryside here is very interesting.

Cleugh is a word meaning steep valley or ravine, and there are many other cleughs not far from Hartleycleugh, mostly pleasant rather than dramatic, but worth seeing. The River West Allen can be reached by following the Hartley Cleugh downstream, to the west. A footpath on the east bank of the river leads north to some picturesque waterfalls by a footbridge. Turning right here leads into the very pleasantly wooded Wolf Cleugh, while across the bridge the path continues towards Farney Cleugh, a deeply cut stream in the open moorland. The heather moorland to the east of Hartleycleugh is Hartley Moor, a gentle hillside where you are unlikely to encounter other walkers. The 574m summit at NY 819 482 is marked by two large cairns, which in this neck of the woods are known as curricks.

Seagull's Welly Pot and Resurgence

Two caves of 20m and 9m
Depth of Pot 13m
Great Limestone
Map: OL 31 – North Pennines
NY 8025 4666 (Pot) and NY 8027 4666 (Resurgence)
Moderate

Introduction
Seagull's Welly Pot in West Allen Dale was first explored by Jimmy Roy, John Dobinson and Neil Woods, of Haymarket Caving Club, in September 1990. The reason for the name is that a used condom was found when boulders were

Seagull's Welly Pot is in a shakehole above this quarry

being removed during exploration, so perhaps the shakehole was already known to enthusiasts of al fresco safe sex.

It is a pleasingly decorated pothole formed in mature limestone, with several chambers connected by narrow rifts. It currently ranks as the second deepest cave in Northumberland, beaten to the title only by Ayleburn Mine Cave, which is currently inaccessible. A 10m electron ladder is recommended for the descent from the entrance to the floor of the first large chamber. The resurgence is a muddy crawl in the quarry that can be visited en route.

The route
Seagull's Welly Pot is above a horseshoe-shaped quarry near the West Allen Dale road between Carrshield and Coalcleugh. Cars can be parked in a small lay-by at NY 804 466 on the east side of the road, opposite the quarry. Cross the road and follow the wall downhill for 100m to a bridge across the River West Allen, then go uphill to the disused quarry.

Seagull's Welly Resurgence
9m
NY 8027 4666

The small stream emanating from the back wall of the quarry is the resurgence from Seagull's Welly Pot. This resurgence can be entered headfirst into a downward-sloping flat-out crawl for 2.5m to a right-angled bend. To the right the flat-out crawl continues for about 3m before straight ahead is too tight. At this point a wriggle over some rocks on the left enters a parallel passage, which presumably connects with Seagull's Welly Pot, but is at present too tight.

There is a hole at the southern end of the quarry wall, which looks promising from a distance but is unfortunately only a very short quarrying excavation with a tiny rift disappearing into nothing from the back wall.

Go up at the southern side of the quarry, and continue to a path that runs along the top of the back wall. Seagull's Welly Pot is at the eastern (downhill) end of an elongated shakehole. A small stream sinks at the western, uphill, end of the shakehole, about 10m from the cave. There are many shakeholes in this area, but the one in which Seagull's Welly Pot is located is quite easy to find, as it is very close to the path that runs along the top of the quarry wall and from the edge of the shakehole, looking back towards the road on the opposite side of the valley, the wall that was followed downhill from the road should appear as a vertical line going straight up the hill.

Seagull's Welly Pot
Length 20m
Depth 13m
NY 8025 4666

The entrance is best treated as a ladder pitch using whatever natural belay you can find. A long stake pushed into the ground will probably be the best bet. Alternatively, it can be free-climbed with care if you feel like a challenge. Get down the fairly narrow entrance and drop into a standing-height chamber. The way on is down a narrow slot in the floor, but it is worth stepping off the ladder at this point to look in the opposite direction, where a narrow rift leads around a corner into a chamber with some aesthetically pleasing speleothems.

Ladder Pitch continues down the slot into a narrow rift, which soon opens out and descends steeply for 7.5m to the floor of a large chamber. The rift straight ahead very quickly becomes too tight, but by climbing back up a short distance two further chambers can be reached. About two metres off the floor a tube leads into Beehive Chamber, which is so named because of its apiarian appearance. The stream at the bottom of this chamber flows through an impassably small connection into the Main Chamber. A welly has been pushed through this connection, but no human or seagull has ever made it through.

A small tube at roof level, 4.5m from the floor of the Ladder Pitch and on the opposite wall from the ladder, is the way into the very impressive Main Chamber. This tube can be entered by straddling the chamber, then the floor of the Main Chamber is reached by making a bold descent down the flowstone ramp, via several small ledges. The walls here are well decorated with flowstone and the stream can be seen through a small hole in the boulder-strewn floor.

Make a day of it

This cave is close to Archbishop Pyrenean Desman Tutu's Welly Pot and many cavers will wish to visit both caves on the same day. It is in an area rich in disused mine workings, many of which will appeal to the intrepid underground explorer. Although it is not within the scope of this book to give detailed descriptions of mine passages, several nearby entrances are quite obvious and some, such as Scaith Hole (no relation) are marked on the Ordnance Survey map. Be very careful if exploring the mines though, as bad air has been reported in this area – a combination of low oxygen and high carbon dioxide levels. The metal-rich water running off from the mines has made the River West Allen one of the most polluted rivers in the UK.

Tutu's Welly Pot

Length 49m
Depth 12m
Great Limestone
Map: OL 31 – North Pennines
NY 8029 4648
Moderate

Introduction
Sometimes you find a new cave and you think you should choose a sensible name for once, but then you go to the pub afterwards and you start coming up with joke names and then everyone prefers the joke name to the sensible name so you're pretty much stuck with that. Well, the full name for this cave is Archbishop Pyrenean Desman Tutu's Welly Pot.

We wanted to use the name Welly because of its proximity to Seagull's Welly Pot, and Kelvin saw a shrew in the shakehole, so we thought about calling it Shrew's Welly Pot. Ben then started telling us about the Pyrenean desman he had seen in the Cantabrian Mountains, and this seemed like a good welly-wearing animal. In the pub later, chaos ensued and the name was changed to Archbishop Pyrenean Desman Tutu's Welly Pot.

The entrance to this cave was found by Ben Coult, of the Moldywarps Speleological Group, in 2015. He went in a couple of metres, but was with some people who were keen to get away, so didn't get far and then forgot about it for a few years. He later told me about the entrance and in August 2017 I went there with a surface team of Ben, plus Kelvin McKivitt of the Durham Cave and Mine Club. Alone underground, I found that there was substantially more to the cave than Ben had originally explored, so I returned a few days later with the same surface team, surveying gear, and my underground companion Alex Ritchie of Black Rose Caving Club, to explore fully.

This cave is of a very different nature to its more mature neighbour, Seagull's Welly Pot. Whilst that cave features well-defined walls in mature limestone, with an obvious route in a top-to-bottom direction, albeit with several chambers, this chossy cave is formed by solution rifts, with plenty of jammed boulders, and numerous short sections of passage. There is water in various parts,

Chris Scaife emerging after the first trip to the bottom of this cave   *Photo by Ben Coult*

dripping down from close to the surface, and it disappears into gravel lower down, without forming any kind of streamway within the cave. Beware of loose rock and be aware that most of the cave is beyond a narrow squeeze.

The route
This cave is very close to Seagull's Welly Pot, so park in the same spot, which is the small lay-by at NY 804 466 on the east side of the West Allen Dale road between Carrshield and Coalcleugh, opposite the horseshoe-shaped quarry. Cross the road and follow the wall downhill for 100m to a bridge across the River West Allen, then follow the river to the south for about 200m until just before a second quarry is reached, at which point there is a lime kiln on the opposite bank. Go uphill to the large shakehole, which is at the end of a long, wide stream bed running down the hill. The pot is in this shakehole.

Climb down the entrance and be careful with the loose rock. There is a small passage leading off towards the falling water, part way down this climb, but the way on is straight down to the bottom of the climb and then through a low section towards a very wet diagonal climb down. This leads into a small dry section, where a too-tight rift ahead connects with a lower chamber. To get into the lower series, there is a narrow squeeze following the water down. Just past this squeeze, a horizontal crawl leads into a dangerously loose chamber and is not recommended. The way on is down to the bottom of this wet climb and into what could almost be described as a dry chamber.

Straight ahead is now a standing-height rift, which slopes downwards to a dead end. A short crawl on the right, at the start of this short rift, leads into the Main Chamber. This chamber, at over 6m high, is quite large for Northumberland and seems to have been formed by another inlet coming from above. This inlet can be reached by an obvious climb up and a higher chamber is visible through a hole in the ceiling.

There are several short thrutchy side passages that can be reached from the floor of the Main Chamber. A squeeze under rocks, low down on the right as you enter the Main Chamber, opens into a small chamber, with barely enough room to sit up. In the Main Chamber, to the left of the inlet that comes from above, the rift continues gently downwards. Straight ahead, at the end of this rift, a mantelshelf leads up to a window on the left, into an awkward bit of passage that chokes after a few metres. On the left, shortly before the end of this rift, is a small passage leading to the deepest point of the cave.

Make a day of it
This cave will usually be combined with a visit to the propinquant Seagull's Welly Pot and its resurgence at the foot of the quarry.

The summit of The Dodd, to the west at NY 791 458, just reaches 2,000 feet (614m) and is only about 1.4km away as the crow flies. The walk to the top is via boggy heather moorland with numerous peat hags, but on a clear day the views from the top are very impressive, with Cross Fell and the Lake District visible to the south-west and the Cheviots to the north.

Elpha Green Caves

Three caves with lengths up to 260m
Great Limestone
Map: OL 31 – North Pennines
NY 8465 4864 to NY 8456 4860
Moderate/Difficult

Introduction

Also known locally as The Elf Holes, caves at Elpha Green have been known about for many years and two caves are described in *Pennine Underground*, with a combined length of 110 feet (33m). In 1971 Peter Ryder, Stuart Hodgson, Alan Holmes and Chris Langthorne, from the Moldywarps Speleological Group, visited and managed to multiply the length of known passage by seven.

East Allen Dale is a remote corner of Northumberland and currently home to three known caves. In addition to the Main Cave, there are two small caves known as Swinhope Burn Cave and Rift Cave. The valley can also boast a number of mines and a ski lift.

There are some impressive formations in the Main Cave, particularly upstream. Some of these are in quite vulnerable positions, so please be very careful not to damage them. The main cave has an active streamway, so may become hazardous and diluvial in wet weather.

The land on which the Swinhope Burn Cave and Main Cave entrances are located currently belongs to the owner of Low Hayrake, more than 1km away in Swin Hope. Permission from the landowner should be obtained prior to any visit. The Rift Cave is in the face of Elphagreen Quarry and permission to access the quarry wall should be sought from Elpha Green Farm. Please be aware that at present it is unlikely that either landowner will grant permission to access the caves.

The route

The Elf Holes are found near Spartylea Bridge, which crosses the River East Allen on the minor road heading west from Spartylea on the B6295, between Allendale Town and Allenheads. Once across Spartylea Bridge, turn right along the minor road, heading north-west towards Allendale Bakery and Elpha Green

Elphagreen Quarry

Cottages. There is a lay-by just after a small second bridge across Swinhope Burn, at NY 848 489.

Follow the burn south, upstream, along a little-used path. After 250m there is a footbridge, but continue south along the west bank of the burn. A short distance south of this footbridge, there is a dry stone wall at the top of the steep bank. Continue south at stream level and soon there will be small rocky outcrops on both sides of the burn, with cave entrances visible under the trees.

Swinhope Burn Cave
8m
NY 8465 4864

On the east bank, a keyhole-shaped entrance leads into this small cave. Swinhope Burn Cave has two entrances and consists of two perpendicular 4m rifts, which cross in the middle and then peter out.

Elpha Green Main Cave
260m
NY 8464 4863

The entrance to Elpha Green Main Cave is in the small outcrop on the west bank, which is often mostly obscured by hawthorn and ivy. Crawl through the entrance and you will reach a spacious aven. To the right is another, smaller entrance. Left from the aven leads to a small slope downwards into some short, narrow passages, none of which goes far. A narrow rift leads to Quarry Entrance, where a large tree now makes the exit difficult for all except very thin lumberjacks.

Returning to the aven just inside the entrance, the way on is an easy crawl down Myxamatosis Passage, which is opposite the Main Entrance. This passage is so named because when first explored there was a dead rabbit in here, and it is likely that several dead rabbits will be seen on any trip into Elpha Green. The passage turns right towards an aven, and then left into a long, low crawl. Opposite this low crawl is a tight connection with the outside world, named Ben's Passage, after Ben Winger, a young local who made the first exit this way in 1999.

The long, low crawl reaches a T-junction with the stream, which is very shallow at this point, and there is a spacious aven. It is best to explore the downstream passage to the right first, as this is much drier than the upstream passage to the left. The passage downstream can be followed via some awkward crawls and small boulder obstacles until daylight coming in from the world can be seen at Ruckle Entrance. It may be possible to emerge here, but the rocks do have a tendency to move together and close this exit.

Upstream from the T-junction, the stream soon becomes deeper and there is a duck straight ahead. Fortunately, for those wishing to stay more or less dry just a bit longer, there is a bypass on the right, via a muddy chamber. This bypass soon rejoins the streamway, with stalactites aplenty. After a short distance, another side passage on the right leads into the very pleasant Penguin Chamber. Back into the streamway, the way upstream continues around a few corners in drier passage, until the final chamber is reached. The cave now continues as a low-airspace canal, known as Feather End, with delicate speleothems hanging down from the ceiling. It is possible, in low water conditions, to reach the end of this, but be very careful not to damage the formations. There is nowhere to turn around in this wet section, so it will need to be reversed carefully.

Elpha Green Rift Cave
9m
NY 8456 4860

There are several fissures in the face of Elphagreen Quarry, which is beside the track leading up to Elpha Green Farm. The longest of these, Rift Cave, is at the western end of the quarry wall and has an entrance crawl to a squeeze up into a small chamber with stalagmites.

Make a day of it

The village of Allenheads, 4km south along the B6295, is a great place to learn about the lead mining industry. There is a heritage centre, open to the public year-round during daylight hours, which includes a traditional blacksmith's shop and a hydraulic engine from Lord Armstrong's day.

If visiting when the snow conditions are good, and water levels are low, it may be possible to make the very rare combination of UK skiing/snowboarding and caving, as there is a ski lift at Allenheads. To find out more, see: **http://ski-allenheads.co.uk/**

The Coast

For the purposes of this book, I have extended the Northumberland coast slightly, as far as the mouth of the Tyne, so as to include the very interesting caves at Cullercoats. Strictly speaking, Cullercoats is in the county of Tyne and Wear, but I hope readers will not object to this addition.

Northumberland is home to several long sandy beaches with a wild and remote feel. For miles of windswept coastal solitude, Druridge Bay, Bamburgh Beach and the north of Lindisfarne are surely amongst the finest beaches in the British Isles. Separating Northumberland's beaches from the outside world, and in many places obscuring them from the view of those passing through by road or rail, are some of the most extensive coastal sand dune systems in the country.

There are wildlife sites of international importance along the coast. Perhaps paramount among these is the archipelago known as the Farne Islands, once home to Saint Aidan and later Saint Cuthbert and now home to large numbers of nesting seabirds, such as puffin and Arctic tern, as well as several thousand grey seals. Boat trips operate to the islands from Seahouses between May and July. The Holy Island of Lindisfarne is renowned for its huge flocks of birds such as pale-bellied brent geese, wigeon and bar-tailed godwit. It is also of great botanical interest with, amongst other rarities, a unique species of orchid. Another excellent seabird site is Coquet Island, where a short boat trip from Amble can take visitors to see almost Britain's entire population of roseate tern, plus England's second largest puffin colony. Whale and dolphin sightings are possible from anywhere along the coast, particularly of harbour porpoise, bottlenose dolphin, white-beaked dolphin and minke whale.

Northumberland can boast more castles than any other English county and some of the most important are found on, or very near, the coastline. Much of the medieval Berwick Castle was demolished to make way for the railway in the 19th century, but the town walls, originally built in the reign of the 'Hammer of the Scots' Edward I, but almost entirely replaced in Tudor times, are often cited as the best-preserved defensive town walls in Britain. A little farther down the coast, picture-postcard Lindisfarne Castle was renovated as a holiday home in the early 20th century and sits in a glorious position on the site of a Tudor fort. The iconic Bamburgh Castle was once the seat of the

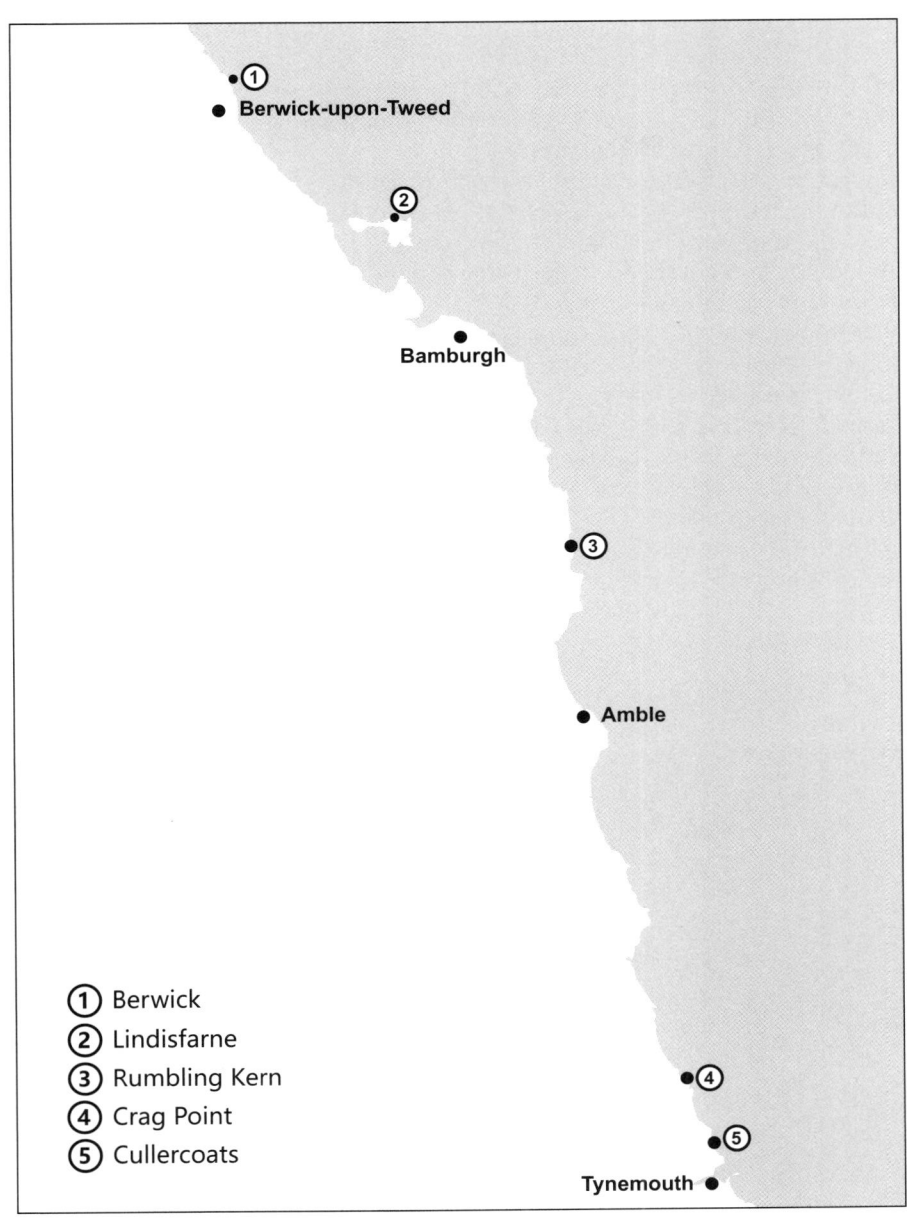

Cave locations on the Coast.

kings of Northumbria, although the building that stands there today was built by the Victorian industrialist Lord Armstrong. Continuing south, the castles at Dunstanburgh, Warkworth and Tynemouth, all managed by English Heritage, offer interesting days out and magnificent views.

For a lucifugous castle experience, the hermitage at Warkworth Castle can be visited in the summer months, by a short ferry ride from the footpath 800m upstream from the castle. The hermitage is a large religious building carved out of the sandstone cliff on the north bank of the River Coquet. It is thought to have been a private chapel built for the first Earl of Northumberland in about 1400.

Rights of way are to be found along most of the coastline; indeed there is a long distance walk known as the Northumberland Coast Path, which stretches 100km from Berwick in the north to Cresswell in the south. Cycling is well catered for as the entire east coast of Great Britain can be cycled via National Cycle Network Route 1, which forms a part of the 6,200km North Sea Cycle Route. The shoreline itself tends to be the property of the Crown and open access is generally allowed for those on foot.

The rocky sections of the Northumberland coast are, for the most part, quite short. However, the caves, cliffs, natural pavements and rock pools are greatly

The coastline north of Berwick, home to many excellent caves

entertaining. The caves in this section are mostly sea caves, also known as littoral caves, that are formed by the wave action of the sea. The floors tend to be made of pebbles, which are thrown around by the incoming tide and contribute to the erosion of the walls. There are some fully submerged caves in the sea, in particular around the Farne Islands, which have not been included in this guidebook as they are permanently underwater. The caves that are included are all on the intertidal shore, and should only be explored at low tide. It is imperative that tide tables are checked in advance before making any journey to visit coastal caves. The BBC website is a very useful online resource for checking tide tables:
http://www.bbc.co.uk/weather/coast_and_sea/tide_tables
Other tide table online resources are available.

BERWICK-UPON-TWEED SEA CAVES

Forty-three caves with lengths up to 67m
Sandstone
Map: 346 – Berwick-upon-Tweed
NU 0033 5391 to NT 9824 5711
Easy to Moderate

Introduction

Berwick-upon-Tweed is famous as a disputed territory that changed hands numerous times during the medieval Anglo-Scottish wars. To the north of Berwick, close to the Scottish border, is a section of coastline with impressive cliffs and a very large number of caves, including by far the longest and most spectacular sea caves in Northumberland. This section of coastline has long been justly popular with sea kayakers, who down the years have visited many of these caves at high tide. They have not previously been recorded in detail though, so I made a number of trips to this area in 2017, sometimes solo and sometimes with fellow Black Rose caver Carolina Smith de la Fuente.

The tides can rise quickly here and some of these caves fill with water at high tide. It is advised that visits are only attempted during calm, settled weather and it is generally best to be on the coastline ready to explore these caves a few hours before low tide and aim to be away from the coastline by an hour or two after low tide. There are long sections of cliff here that would be very difficult or impossible to climb up if caught by a rising tide, so unless you are willing to wade or swim a long distance back do not linger.

That said, this section of coastline will provide a very entertaining experience for well-prepared, bold readers. There are myriad small clefts, rifts and hollows in these cliffs that have been omitted as they are not quite long enough, but feel free to explore these extra holes.

The route

Because of the ebb and flow, it is not possible to visit all of the caves here on foot in a single day. For this reason, I have divided them into three walks. If in doubt about the rising tide, there is no shame in cutting short any of these walks. The two caves closest to Berwick are accessible at all times except for extremely high tide, so can be visited whenever you like.

The Berwickshire Coastal Path provides very pleasant, straightforward access to the coast north of Berwick, so all routes start at the same point, which is a free car park at Green's Haven, NU 002 536, between the Magdalene Fields golf course and Berwick Holiday Park. The Magdalene Fields is a large area that takes its name from a hospital that was built here in the Middle Ages and dedicated to Mary Magdalene. Northumberland Avenue, the road that runs from the A1167 to Magdalene Fields, passes the medieval town wall. Keep your eyes on the road of course, but try not to miss the octagonal Bell Tower, built on an older base in 1577.

Rail travellers can easily get to the Green's Haven car park, as the railway station is located at the top of Northumberland Avenue. If walking from the railway station, walk north up the road a short distance to the mini roundabout and follow Northumberland Avenue down towards the holiday park. From Berwick Holiday Park entrance, follow the path east towards the sea.

Green's Haven Caves
Easy

These short caves are close to the parking spot and usually accessible whatever the tidal situation. As such, they can easily be combined with any of the three main walks.

Follow the steps down to the beach from the Green's Haven car park (NU 002 536) and turn left, heading north. There is an old bathing pool on this beach. About 300m from the car park, there are some steps heading up to the holiday park. A very small cave is found just before these steps and a longer cave, Green's Haven Cave 1, is right underneath them.

Green's Haven Cave 1
8m
NU 0033 5391

This narrow rift is formed by a large boulder, leaning against the cliff face, and offers a thrutchy transition from the comfort of the sandy beach to the more exciting rocky shore. Go straight through this cave to leave the sand behind and arrive on the rocks.

Green's Haven Cave 2
8m
NU 0034 5393

Just 15m up the coast from Cave 1 is a bell-shaped entrance with a sandy floor. Turn right in here to exit through a tube. A few metres farther on, there is a short, flat-out 2.5m cave.

Walk One – Farthest North
Easy

These caves are on drier land and less affected by the tide than those in Walks Two and Three, but it is still recommended to visit at low tide.

To get to the caves north of the spectacular rock arch known as Needle's Eye, follow the Berwickshire Coastal Path north from the Green's Haven car park (NU 002 536) for 3.9km. The path is easy to follow and remains close to the clifftops for its entire length, offering excellent views of the coastline and out to sea. After 2.6km, at NT 995 552, there is an excellent viewpoint towards Needle's Eye up the coast to the north.

After following the Berwickshire Coastal Path for 3.9km, the path briefly goes up alongside the railway embankment. At this point, NT 987 561, a small valley, with some short, exposed sandstone walls on its southern side, points towards the sea. Head carefully down to the shore from here along a path, via an old metal ladder and around a right-angled rock face.

There are several caves on the stretch of coast known as St John's Haven, between here and Needle's Eye. Turn right and walk south down the coast, passing a very tall and wide rock shelter, at NT 9889 5596, and then a jumble of boulders at NT 9898 5585, which contains some very small caves.

St John's Haven Cave 1
17m
NT 9905 5570

Under an enormous overhang 25m wide and 11m high. A passage towards the left end of the overhang goes back 17m in total from the rock face.

St John's Haven Cave 2
40m
NT 9909 5560

This is a gigantic cave. The trapezoidal entrance is 12m wide and 9m high, and this width is maintained all the way to the back wall. The floor is comprised of large rocks and there is much driftwood at the back of the cave. A very small passage, currently filled in with stones, leads off to the right from the back wall.

The cliff between here and Needle's Eye contains numerous small holes, depressions, tubes, rifts etc. Most only go in a short distance, but one is long enough for its own entry in this book.

St John's Haven Cave 3
10m
NT 9919 5556

Up some slippery rocks, this short saturnine passage has a low ceiling and deep rock pools. Only aim to reach the end if you're happy to get very wet and muddy.

Needle's Eye Cave
15m
NT 9923 5553

The sea level is always fairly deep beneath the striking Needle's Eye natural archway, even at low tide. However, an adventurous passage, reached by a short, slippery climb up the rock in the right-angled corner where the projection meets the cliff, leads into a gently descending rift onto a large serene platform within this great arch.

To get to the northernmost caves in England, retrace your steps along the shore and past the right-angled rock face, then continue north towards Marshall Meadows Bay. There are some dramatic rock formations just south of the bay and a stream emerges from a man-made hole in the cliff at NT 9832 5659. I would never wish to discourage anyone from looking for caves, but I was unable to find anything in this part that made the nettle stings worthwhile.

A 75m man-made tunnel is passed at NT 9818 5673. This tunnel was carved out of the rock in the 1830s, when the railway was built, and was used to haul seaweed up from the shore, to be used as agricultural fertiliser. Today it provides a very entertaining route between Marshall Meadows Bay and the caravan park above, with a fixed rope for a handline throughout its length, which is handy as the floor can get very slippery. In situ ropes and ladders can be used to access the tunnel from the rocky shore.

The coastline to the north of the tunnel, with vegetation hanging down the walls, looks quite exotic, as if you are approaching foreign lands.

Marshall Meadows Cave
8m
NT 9817 5703

Walk north alongside the cliff, which is overhanging for much of its length. About 300m as the crow flies from the exit to the tunnel, the first cave is found up a 3m climb onto a ledge with a jumble of rocks, in a fairly wide opening in the rock face. There are several other concavities very close to this. The cave has a flat-floored entrance and begins very low, with just enough room to kneel towards the back. There are several small stalactites in this cave.

Alt Nan Uamh Alba Na Fàg Mi
5m
NT 9824 5711

Just around the corner of Marshall Meadows Point, there is a crack in the rock face. This section of cliff appears to have slipped apart, with the layers on the left-hand side noticeably tilted. This has created the most northerly cave in England. It has quite a large entrance, but soon lowers. At the back there is a tiny passage sloping upwards for a short distance. This cave's name is inspired by a line from the Jonny and the Baptists song, *Scotland Don't Leave Me*.

These are all just artificial borders made long ago to increase the power of a select few and create dissonance amongst the proletariat, but nonetheless this is a book about the Caves of Northumberland, so our journey north ends here. The best way to return from here to Green's Haven is to go back along the beach and through the 75m tunnel, then rejoin the Berwickshire Coastal Path by a ladder stile from the caravan park. It is then a 4.8km walk back along the clifftop path.

Alt Nan Uamh Alba Na Fàg Mi

Walk Two – Burgess' Cove and Brotherston's Hole
Easy/Moderate

This trip involves visiting a large number of caves that are all close together. If the tide tables have been consulted, and wellies are worn, it should be possible to stay more or less dry for most of the caves; however, to see every nook and cranny here getting wet will be necessary, so a wetsuit will be a great advantage.

From the Green's Haven car park, NU 002 536, follow the Berwickshire Coastal Path north up the coastline for about 700m and after winding around Sharpers' Head, a small sandy beach is reached. Steps, at NU 001 541, lead down from the holiday park to the southern end of this beach and a stream enters on the left from Dodd's Well near the northern end. The large cave entrances in the south-facing cliff of Burgess' Cove are obvious from this beach. At low tide the ground in front of this south-facing cliff contains many rock pools. It should be noted that this area will be affected rapidly by the rising tide and there may be deep water between here and the beach when there is still plenty of dry ground around the corner to the north.

Burgess' Cove 1
44m
NU 0007 5439

This cave, which is a popular pigeon roost, has a large entrance, slightly raised from the level of the rocky shore. The tall passage cuts straight into the cliff face for 12m. Half way in, there is a cross rift: left is walking height for 22m; right is a passage across deep pools of water, which is connected to Burgess' Cove 2, but becomes impassably tight after 10m.

Burgess' Cove 2
8m
NU 0008 5439

The next cave, 10m farther east, has a large, keyhole-shaped entrance at the same height as Burgess' Cove 1. Step up onto the ledge and follow a roomy passage to a flat back wall. To the left is the impassable connection to the neighbouring cave.

Burgess' Cove 3
15m
NU 0011 5440

Just before the corner of Burgess' Cove, there is this wide entrance into a cave that arcs around and cuts the corner. There is a fairly deep rock pool for almost the entire length of this cave and it is very difficult indeed to stay completely dry if making the through trip. The floor rises towards the roof, making a crawling-height exit.

Proceeding north, at NU 0011 5447, 70m from the corner of Burgess' Cove is a rock shelter 19m wide and 2m high, with the back wall 2.5m back from the cliff edge.

Magdalene Cave 1
11m
NU 0011 5450

About 30m north of the rock shelter is this rocky-floored cave with a bell-shaped entrance. There is an interesting archway 30m farther up the coast.

Magdalene Cave 2
15m
NU 0012 5458

Another 40m up the coast from the archway is this cave with a very impressive entrance, 16m wide and 7m high.

Magdalene Cave 3
31m
NU 0013 5461

Just around a corner, 30m from the previous cave, is this interesting site. The first 13m is a tall and wide passage with several rock pools, which can be traversed around with care. The passage then bends to the right and drier going over boulders leads to a back wall with a pebbled floor.

Magdalene Cave 4
6m
NU 0012 5464

This cave has a tall triangular entrance and is to the right of another, similar-shaped but much shallower, opening in the cliff. There is a rock pool in the entrance, which can be stepped around and the cave remains walking height to the back wall.

Magdalene Cave 5
9m
NU 0011 5465

Just before the corner leading round to a small cove, a choice of smaller or larger entrance leads into a narrow passage that gives a through trip, emerging beside a concrete structure with a pipe coming out.

An escape route can be followed by climbing up the left-hand side of this concrete structure, to reach a small path that soon connects with the Berwickshire Coastal Path. The next six serried cave entrances are on the face heading immediately north from this climbable construction.

Magdalene Cave 6
13m
NU 0009 5465

This impressive cave, visible from the Berwickshire Coastal Path, has an entrance 6m wide and 5m high. The passage maintains these dimensions, more or less, all the way to the end.

Magdalene Cave 7
12m
NU 0009 5466

This is a more unassuming entrance between the two much larger caves. A short climb up leads into a crawl.

Magdalene Cave 8
19m
NU 0009 5467

A very spacious cave, with the entrance 9m wide and 6m high. There are rock pools inside, but these can easily be avoided.

Looking out from Magdalene Cave 8

Magdalene Cave 9
10m
NU 0009 5468

Walk up a ramp into this triangular entrance. From the top of the ramp, there is a slippery climb down into a pool with water well above the knee, leading to the exit. This pool is quite large and continues into the entrance to the next cave, although the water gets above waist deep to get to it.

Magdalene Cave 10
10m
NU 0009 5470

Wading or swimming in the deep pool is required to get to this triangular entrance. Although the approach is very wet, the back of the cave is dry and sandy.

There is a fantastic archway between Caves 10 and 11.

Magdalene Cave 11
17m
NU 0009 5471

Just past the archway, a large entrance with a rock pool that can be avoided if necessary, leads into a passage that bends to the right.

The next three caves are found around the corner from the previous cave, in a sheltered cove known as Brotherston's Hole. The rocks in this area are covered with seaweed and very slippery.

Brotherston's Hole Cave 1
12m
NU 0006 5473

Large rectangular entrance formed by an overhang. Walk in for 8m to the back wall. A stooping passage on the right, just inside the entrance, is 4m long and provides an alternative exit.

Brotherston's Hole Cave 2
8m
NU 0003 5473

An entrance 16m wide and 4m high, at the back wall of the cove, soon closes down. The floor is made up of smooth rocks.

Brotherston's Hole Cave 3
42m
NU 0003 5474

A small triangular hole in the north wall of the cove is the beginning of this magnificent through trip. A great passage cuts a straight line through the rock, with an average width of about 4m and an average height of more than 5m. The large rock pools on the floor can mostly be avoided by scrambling around the edges, until the final pool at the North Entrance, where the water will be about knee-deep.

Brotherston's Hole Cave 4
8m
NU 0003 5477

This cave is on the section of cliff that would be missed out if one were to complete the through trip in Cave 3 and then just plough on north. When walking up the coast from the South Entrance of Cave 3 a tantalising rift can be seen up a difficult climb. Fortunately, just around the corner, a much easier climb provides a back-door entry, as it were, into this rift.

Just before the corner that leads around to the North Entrance of Cave 3, a climb up leads into a tiny passage that enters Cave 3 high up. However, the connection is too tight. Past the North Entrance there is another promising looking crack quite high up the cliff, but it does not go far.

Brotherston's Hole Cave 5
8m
NT 9999 5481

Another fine archway, a feature in which these cliffs excel, is entered by climbing up a slippery ramp and exited by descending an entirely different slippery ramp.

Brotherston's Hole Cave 6
6m
NT 9998 5481

Very close to Cave 5, the wide entrance is broken by a 'column'. Climbing up slippery walls leads to a low, greasy section.

Brotherston's Hole Cave 7
24m
NT 9996 5483

An enormous rectangular entrance, 6m high and 13m wide, ensures that daylight persists throughout this cave. Walk in along the bouldery floor. The cave bends slightly to the right at the back.

Brotherston's Hole Cave 8
9m
NT 9995 5484

The overhang that forms the ceiling of Cave 7 continues along the cliff to make this complex rock shelter, which again has a wide entrance. Scramble up to reach the back wall.

Caves 9 and 10 are side by side and have large, almost circular entrances.

Brotherston's Hole Cave 9
9m
NT 9991 5487

The back of this cave is reached by an easy walk up the slope, then a climb up the green wall into a short flat-out crawl.

Brotherston's Hole Cave 10
9m
NT 9990 5487

This very spacious cave, with an entrance 6m high and 7m wide, is reached by traversing above a rock pool.

A little further along the coast is a large triangular entrance, which regrettably does not lead into very much of a cave. However, there is one more noteworthy cave coming up before the beach, and anyone tiring of slippery climbs will be pleased to know that this one starts at ground level.

Brotherston's Hole Cave 11
15m
NT 9984 5491

Two large entrances unite to make this a well-lit cave. There is a wonderful natural rock-bridge below the ceiling.

Further up the coast, at NT 998 549, is a sandy beach. A little path up the steep grassy bank behind the beach will take you back to the Berwickshire Coastal Path. Follow this for 2km to return to Green's Haven.

Walk Three – The Aquatic Ones
Moderate

The caves on this beautiful section of coast are rarely visited without a boat, as there is no dry route to them. This is certainly no perambulation, but with preparation, sartorial pragmatism and an intrepid approach, speleological souls can enter paradise unferried.

The best access point for these caves is the sandy beach at NT 998 549, reached by following the Berwickshire Coastal Path north from Green's Haven car park (NU 002 536) for about 2km, then following a steep path down the grassy slope. Now turn left and head north.

Jutting Arch
10m
NT 9950 5528

This archway is found on the rocky coastline north of the beach, tucked against the wall behind a large, distinctive projection that otherwise blocks the way on.

The Last Hearth
11m
NT 9945 5527

Just around a corner, which welly-wearers may be able to navigate without getting completely soaked, is this tall, wide entrance formed by an overhang 9m above. Climb up large boulders to the back, where the cave narrows. The name is a reference to the relative comfort of this cave, which juxtaposes with the approaching mandatory immersion.

A little farther along the coast, at NT 9937 5529, there is an interesting blowhole-like feature at the top of the cliff.

It is not possible to stay dry if visiting the caves from here to Needle's Eye, even at low tide. Anyone keen to explore these caves needs to be prepared to get completely soaked. A wetsuit, and summer visit, is advised.

Mashu Tunnel
67m
NT 9934 5532

Swimming, or if the tide is very low, chest-deep wading, is required to reach this grand entrance. This is a marvellous through trip with the passage dimensions on average 7m high and 4m wide. There is deep water for most of the way, but whatever you're wearing will be sodden by now, so don't worry

Chris Scaife by the entrance to Mashu Tunnel
Photo by Carolina Smith de la Fuente

about that. Mashu, of course, is the Great Cedar Mountain through which Gilgamesh journeyed to reach the paradisiacal Garden of the Gods at the edge of the world.

Garden of the Gods Cave 1
15m
NT 9929 5536

After emerging from Mashu Tunnel into the Garden of the Gods, a delightful secluded cove, turn right and shortly you will reach this rift 4m high and about 80cm wide. There is usually waist-deep water in the cave, even at low tide.

Garden of the Gods Cave 2
17m
NT 9924 5537

At the back wall of this spectacular cove, an enormous overhang, and popular convenience for our feathered friends, creates this cave. Despite the otherwise idyllic situation, a certain amount of flotsam, jetsam and avian guano needs to be crossed in order to reach the end.

Singing Cove
32m
NT 9924 5541

This commodious cave is around a promontory in the next secluded cove. The bell-shaped entrance is 17m high and 19m wide. Not quite a Saint Paul's Cathedral, but it's a large one.

Around another promontory there is a bay immediately south of Needle's Eye.

Needle's Eye Bay Cave 1
60m
NT 9923 5546

The southernmost cave in the bay is this spectacular tubular passage, with an entrance 8m wide and 7m high. Wade in through water for the first 36m, then the cave opens out into a dry chamber, with a small alcove on the left-hand side of the back wall.

Needle's Eye Bay Cave 2
37m
NT 9923 5549

Just north of Cave 1, the entrance to this cave has similar dimensions, but with a tall, narrow passage leading into the darkness. After walking through shallow water, the cave opens out into a large dry chamber, 10m wide and 3m high.

Needle's Eye Bay Cave 3
21m
NT 9924 5551

Before the corner of the bay there is another wide entrance. Walk in across relatively dry boulders to the back wall.

Needle's Eye Bay Cave 4
6m
NT 9927 5551

This short, entertaining, through trip is on the corner just before Needle's Eye. Through a large round hole is a tricky climb up, followed by a gentle ramp down to a pool.

Make a day of it

When the tide is coming in, it is best to get away from the shore. The Berwickshire Coastal Path stretches 48km from Berwick-upon-Tweed to Cockburnspath in the north. This path is well-waymarked and allows the coastline – or at least the ground just inland of the coastline – north of Berwick-upon-Tweed to be explored with relative ease. There is much impressive coastal scenery to be enjoyed by following this trail to the north as far as you wish.

To see Berwick's ramparts, follow the Berwickshire Coastal Path to the south, walking between the cliffs and the golf course, with fences on either side. The path descends onto a minor road, which takes you to the Cowport gateway – a tunnel through the walls, which was one of the original Tudor gates into the town. Once through, head up onto the walls and enjoy. The ramparts are open year-round and access is free. The path circumnavigating Berwick is easy to follow and affords excellent views. There are many places of historical interest to see along the way, such as the barracks, Holy Trinity Parish Church, Berwick Castle and several bastions. Berwick is a delightful town that is well worth visiting at leisure.

LINDISFARNE CAVES

Eight caves with lengths up to 15m
Limestone
Map: 340 – Holy Island and Bamburgh
NU 1287 4378 to NU 1301 4384
Easy

Introduction

The Holy Island of Lindisfarne is a fascinating place. During the 7th century the monastery founded here by the Irish monk Saint Aidan was perhaps the most important Christian site in the whole of England and it became the seat of the most famous Bishop of Lindisfarne – Saint Cuthbert, patron saint of Northumbria – in the year 685. Leaving wealthy, unarmed settlements by the coast may have been the downfall of the Saxons however, who left themselves vulnerable to attacks by sea. The Viking raid of Lindisfarne in 793 is widely regarded as the beginning of the Viking Age in Western Europe.

Today the island is a popular tourist destination linked to the mainland at low tide by a causeway. Two long distance walks, St Cuthbert's Way and St Oswald's Way, culminate on the island, after making the pilgrimage across the causeway.

The caves on Lindisfarne have been known about for many centuries and it is said that the monks even in Aidan's day would retreat to this bay for spiritual cogitation. The bay in which they are found, though marked on most modern maps as Coves Haven, was formerly known as Caves Haven. Early descriptions of Caves Haven refer to 'dark and yawning caverns' with entrances of great width. The caves have been greatly reduced because of large-scale quarrying in the mid 19th century, when limestone from Nessend Quarry was transported by waggonway to lime kilns elsewhere on the island. William Weaver Tomlinson, a historian who wrote several books about Northumberland in the 19th century, lamented the destruction of the 'interesting limestone caverns', which he said were 'being destroyed by the utilitarian aggressor'. Today, we are left with mere remnants of the pre-industrial landscape.

The causeway leading to the Holy Island of Lindisfarne can only be crossed at certain times. Please search http://www.northumberland.gov.uk/ for safe crossing times.

The route

Park in the large car park at NU 126 424. Follow the road south towards the village for 370m, then turn left, signposted 'St Aidan's RC Church'. Another 150m farther on, after passing the church and the disabled car park, with public toilets, head left at a T-junction towards St Coombs Farm. About 200m along this road, after passing St Coombs Farmhouse, the tarmac road ends but a large track, known as the Straight Lonnen, continues north, signposted 'Public Right of Way'. Follow this track for 1km to a gate entering the sand dunes in Lindisfarne National Nature Reserve. The path to the right continues as a fantastic circuit of the island, passing the lough and the castle. The path to the coast is quite faint, but keep heading north and after 600m you will arrive at the beach at Coves Haven. The caves are on the cliff face to the right, and are numbered from south-west to north-east. This is an area rich in wildlife, and particularly good for grey seals.

Lindisfarne Cave 1
5m
NU 1287 4378

The short first cave has a wide entrance and funnels inwards.

Lindisfarne Cave 2
8m
NU 1294 4382

A fairly small triangular hole under a large overhang leads into this rocky-floored cave, which is flat-out at the end. This is about 80m from Cave 1, but the remaining caves are all quite close together.

Lindisfarne Cave 3
15m
NU 1296 4383

This one has a very tall entrance. The ceiling remains high for most of its length and there is a rocky floor that slopes upwards to the back.

Lindisfarne Cave 4
5m
NU 1297 4384

Very close to Cave 3 and 2m in from the cliff edge is a slippery 2m climb up into a 3m alcove. This cave is beneath an impressive overhang.

Lindisfarne Cave 5
4m
NU 1298 4384

Just around the corner and up a slippery 2.5m climb is this crouching-height, 4m cave.

Lindisfarne Cave 6
6m
NU 1300 4384

Beside a small natural arch, a wide cave with a rocky floor, which remains walking height to the back.

Lindisfarne Cave 7
8m
NU 1301 4384

A large entrance into a wide walking passage, just past Cave 6.

View from inside Lindisfarne Cave 6

Lindisfarne Cave 8
5m
NU 1301 4385

The small triangular entrance to the last cave on this stretch of coastline is very close to Cave 7. A small chamber opens out beyond the entrance.

Make a day of it

Exploring the coastline in either direction will not disappoint, unless the tide comes in and you get swept out to sea. For a circuit of the island, head back south for 600m to rejoin the public footpath heading east. Follow this path for about 2km to the splendid Lindisfarne Castle via the east coast. Just north of the castle is a very interesting garden designed by Gertrude Jekyll. Follow the road west from the castle for 1km to return to the village, where there are several pubs and cafes to choose from as well as Lindisfarne Priory. The priory, an English Heritage site, is a dramatic ruin with an excellent museum.

Alternatively, for a more remote experience, head west along the north coast of the island, following the dunes for just over 2km to get to the Snook. The coastline here varies greatly depending on the tides, but at low tide the huge expanse to the north and west is breathtaking.

Rumbling Kern Caves

Three caves with lengths up to 33m
Sandstone
Map: 332 – Alnwick and Amble
NU 2622 1727 to NU 2623 1724
Easy

Introduction
Rumbling Kern is a wonderful coastal feature where the powerful flow of the sea has carved a great tunnel through the rock, with a steep-sided pool beyond, into which the tides rumble and churn. In addition to Rumbling Kern itself, there are a couple of other caves to enjoy in the vicinity. The caves here have been known about for many years, and are sometimes visited by kayakers and local outdoor pursuits centres, but they had not previously been described to the caving world until I visited with Carolina Smith de la Fuente of Black Rose Caving Club in 2015.

This site is located just to the south of a bathing house made for the family of Charles Grey, the second Earl Grey, who succeeded the Duke of Wellington as prime minister of the United Kingdom. Earl Grey's government introduced the Great Reform Act and abolished slavery in the British Empire, but he is probably best known as the inspiration for the name of a flavoured tea. The home of the Grey family is the nearby Howick Hall.

As with most sea caves, these caves should only ever be visited at low tide. It is worth arriving a couple of hours before low tide, to allow enough time to enjoy the caves and the beach in this fascinating location.

The route
Park at NU 259 174 near Seahouses Farm, Howick, and follow the public footpath for 300m to the beach. Turn right and walk down the beach, where the quarried sandstone forms small cliffs that face inland to create a very tranquil sheltered cove. A scramble over the rocks at the southern end of this beach leads to the descent into Rumbling Kern, a pool connected to the sea by a 10m tunnel. A second scramble, continuing south, leads to Rumbling Kern Cave and Rumbling Kern Archway.

Rumbling Kern *Photo by Carolina Smith de la Fuente*

Rumbling Kern
10m
NU 2622 1727

A wide tunnel, 10m long, leads to the sea from a depression in a rocky section just south of the sandy beach. On the right at the opening of the tunnel is a perpendicular 8m passage.

To get from Rumbling Kern to Rumbling Kern Cave, scramble over a sandstone outcrop. When climbing down, Rumbling Kern Cave is on the right-hand side at the corner of the cliff.

Rumbling Kern Cave
33m
NU 2622 1725

This surprisingly long cave has a narrow, rectangular entrance in the corner of a short cliff face. It starts as a 9m walking passage to a junction. Straight ahead is a squeeze, best tackled standing upright, followed by 13m of passage, bending right and lowering towards the end. The right-hand passage from the junction is an 11m crawl.

Rumbling Kern Archway
7m
NU 2623 1724

On a large rock projection between Rumbling Kern Cave and the sea is an archway, carpeted with boulders, which can be walked through at low tide.

Make a day of it

The 2km or so of coastline north up the coast from here is one of the best places in Northumberland to find fossils. The best section of beach for fossils starts roughly 500m north of Rumbling Kern, where large sandstone blocks contain plant fossils, including the impressions of tree trunks. A little farther north, there is more limestone, mudstone and shale, containing a wide variety of fossils, such as brachiopods, crinoids and trilobites. Please note however that this is a SSSI (Site of Special Scientific Interest) so it is not permitted to break the bedrock.

The Northumberland Coastal Path is worth following in either direction from Rumbling Kern. If heading north, after about 2km you will reach the cliffs at Cullernose Point, home to nesting kittiwakes. These cliffs are part of the Whin Sill – a great layer of the igneous rock dolerite, which stretches across the North East of England and includes outcrops at High Force and several parts of Hadrian's Wall, as well as Lindisfarne, Bamburgh and Dunstanburgh Castles. There are a couple of very short caves in the cliffs of Swine Den, just south of Cullernose Point. After another 1km you will get to the picturesque fishing village of Craster, famed for its kippers. A further 2km up the coast is the ruin of Dunstanburgh Castle, in the care of English Heritage and open to the public. Check the website for opening times and further information:
http://www.english-heritage.org.uk/visit/places/dunstanburgh-castle/

CRAG POINT CAVES

Eight caves with lengths up to 35m
Sandstone
Map: 316 – Newcastle upon Tyne
NZ 3433 7625 to NZ 3435 7615
Easy

Introduction
South of the industrial town of Blyth, the long golden sands of South Beach stretch down the coast for 4.5km to the small port of Seaton Sluice. Continuing southwards, there is about 3km of rocky shore between Seaton Sluice and St Mary's Island and within this stretch of rocky coastline, several caves are to be found at Crag Point. South of St Mary's Island, there is another stretch of sandy beach at Whitley Sands, which stretches down towards Whitley Bay.

The rocky section of coastline has been the scene of many shipwrecks throughout history. One notable story is that of Thomas Langley, who was awarded the Royal Humane Society's bronze medal for his daring rescue in 1880. He was voluntarily lowered about 20m down the cliff on a rope to rescue the crew of a Dutch galliot, which had run aground in a storm, with the captain swept out to sea and drowned. Langley saved all aboard – the captain's wife and child, as well as two helpless hands. The Seaton Sluice Watch House Museum, on the site of the headquarters of the Seaton Sluice Volunteer Life-Saving Company, tells the story of many such shipwrecks and also contains a permanent display of local historical photographs. It is currently open to the public on Sunday afternoons in the summer.

These caves should only be visited at low tide. Several hours either side of high tide, the entrances will be inaccessible on foot.

The route
Cars can be parked on Collywell Bay Road in Seaton Sluice, at NZ 340 762. A footpath leads east from here and soon loops down to the shore, which can be followed to the east. There are a few very small caves on this north-facing stretch of shoreline, but the main caves at Crag Point begin at the rocky promontory. The caves are numbered from the farthest north, with Cave 1

being right on the promontory. The southernmost cave is found close to the point where the crag gets much lower. The caves here are all quite close together, so once Cave 1 has been found, just follow the line of the crag southwards along the rocky shore and the others will be found easily.

Crag Point Cave 1
35m
NZ 3433 7625

The large entrance in the rock buttress leads into a passage over 3m high. Even at low tide, there is an 8m long pool, 14m into the cave. If careful, this can be traversed without getting your feet wet. The pool is followed by a pebble slope, which rises to the back of the cave.

Crag Point Cave 2
20m
NZ 3432 7624

This cave is at the corner where the rocky promontory ends and the cliff starts to run south. A wide entrance on the right is the way in to a cobble slope up

Don Miller beside Crag Point Cave 1

to a square passage. There is a 4m long passage to the left of the main part of the cave.

Crag Point Cave 3
25m
NZ 3432 7622

An opening 2.7m wide and 3.5m high, reached by climbing over boulders. The tall walking passage ends at a wall, but if you are keen to carry on there is an extra 2m of flat-out crawling at floor level. A separate climb up to the left of the main entrance joins the main cave after 5m.

Crag Point Cave 4
8m
NZ 3434 7618

A high, wide entrance, which separates into a small hole on the right and a tall, narrow rift on the left.

Crag Point Cave 5
6m
NZ 3434 7617

A just off-vertical narrow rift. There is another rift 2m to the south, which is narrower and tilting slightly in the opposite direction.

Crag Point Cave 6
11m
NZ 3435 7617

Similar in appearance to Cave 5, with bilateral off-vertical fissures. The opening on the right, reached by climbing some large boulders, is the way in.

Crag Point Cave 7
10m
NZ 3435 7616

A tall passage reached by a slippery boulder.

Crag Point Cave 8
4m
NZ 3435 7615

A tall, wide entrance with walls that narrow towards the back.

Make a day of it

The coastal path above Crag Point, or the rocky shoreline itself at low tide, can be followed south for 1.8km to the lighthouse on St Mary's Island. This is a deservedly popular tourist spot, connected to the coast at low tide by a causeway. The island is a Local Nature Reserve with important bird populations and the lighthouse, built in 1898, contains a visitor centre that is open year-round.

The Watch House Museum is found at the northern end of Collywell Bay Road, behind The King's Arms pub. To get to another nearby Local Nature Reserve, known as Holywell Dene, follow Collywell Bay Road north to the very end, then cross the A193 to St Paul's Church at NZ 336 767. A footpath follows the path of Seaton Burn through the dene. This dene begins as a tidal flood plain, as far as the village of Hartley, then becomes steep-sided ancient woodland either side of Seaton Burn, before reaching the village of Holywell.

The National Trust property Seaton Delaval Hall is also nearby, at NZ 322 766, and can be reached either by road or by walking up the dismantled railway from Holywell Dene at NZ 325 748. There is more information on the website: **https://www.nationaltrust.org.uk/seaton-delaval-hall**

Cullercoats Caves

Six caves with lengths up to 19m
Sandstone
Map: 316 – Newcastle upon Tyne
NZ 3661 7111 to NZ 3637 7125
Easy

Introduction

The caves closest to the city of Newcastle upon Tyne are found on the coast at Cullercoats, between North Tyneside's flagship coastal resorts, Whitley Bay and Tynemouth. Technically these caves are in Tyne and Wear, not Northumberland, so think of this as a bonus track. Any readers who object to their inclusion on geographical grounds should delay their visit until the publication of the tome *The Caves of Tyne and Wear*. Cullercoats Bay is a very picturesque sandy bay with cliffs and easily accessible caves. Unusually for caves in this guide, or indeed any caving guide, they are very close to a Metro station.

The caves are near the great geological fault known as the Ninety Fathom Dyke. This is a major slip-dyke that continues a vast distance underground and has displaced coal measures along the way, at Gosforth, Blaydon and Carlisle.

As with many sea caves near populated areas, stories of smuggling abound. Customs officer Captain Thomas Armstrong, known as the 'Smuggler King of Cullercoats', lived in Cliff House, originally known as Bank Top House, on Victoria Crescent in the late 18th century. He was dismissed from his job in 1776 for allowing two notorious smugglers to escape justice and it was found that he had been imprisoning smugglers, and storing their smuggled goods, in his cellar. A trapdoor in the study of his house led into a secret passage that connected with the beach. This is now blocked by the defensive walls that were built in the 1960s.

People have been visiting these caves for many years. An article published in *Newcastle Magazine* in 1823 describes a skylight in the top of Smuggler's Cave, through which at high tide the furious sea could be heard to roar, 'like the subterranean firing of a file of musketry'. This skylight has since been blocked by rockfall, much to the dismay of nostalgic musketeers.

Tynemouth Priory and Castle stand to the south of Cullercoats on a magnesian limestone headland. This is an isolated example of the rock type that makes up much of the coastline from South Shields to Hartlepool, and south of the Tyne contains several excellent sea caves. The magnesian limestone at Tynemouth is home to the legendary Jingling Geordie's Hole, previously known as Jingling Man's Hole, a man-made hollow on the cliff-face below Tynemouth Priory, but with its entrance apparently blocked by rockfall in 1836. Inside were two dungeons and a well-like cavity.

According to legend, Jingling Geordie was a 17th century pirate and smuggler who lured ships onto the rocks at the Black Middens, south of the castle, and would plunder the wrecks, then hide the loot in the labyrinth of tunnels beneath the castle. He is called Jingling Geordie because he had fetters wrapped around his legs and his ghost's chains jingle on the castle walls on spooky dark nights. Another legend speaks of the 'Witche of Tinmouth', who inhabited this cave, and yet another tells of Walter the Bold, the son of a valiant knight, who sought to emulate his father's courage and was told of great treasures in a cave beneath Tynemouth Castle. Walter fought off a host of infernal spirits to acquire much wealth and his father's admiration.

A great cave for storytellers, but regrettably Jingling Geordie's Hole is better imagined than looked for, as the cliffs are currently disappointingly lacking in labyrinths stocked full of pirate plunder and bullion.

The route

Park in the long seafront car park, which runs between Blue Reef Aquarium and St George's C. of E. Church (NZ 365 708). This 19th century church is a Grade I listed building in French Gothic style and is open to visitors.

Alternatively, if using the Tyne and Wear Metro, leave Cullercoats Metro Station and after 30m turn right onto Marsden Terrace. After 150m turn left at the T-junction onto Marsden Avenue, which leads to the seafront at Beverley Terrace. From here you can head straight down into Cullercoats Bay but it is worth walking south along Beverley Terrace for 400m to see St George's Church and the northern part of the beach at Long Sands.

Opposite the church, take the steps leading down onto Long Sands beach, then turn left (north). After 400m you will reach the sandstone crag at Tynemouth North Point, formerly known as George's Point. Both of the caves at Tynemouth North Point are underneath low-angled sandstone and it is easy to scramble above them. They are so close together that they are often treated as a single cave, Smuggler's Cave.

Smuggler's Cave 1
10m
NZ 3661 7111

This fantastic triple archway is 5m high and 9m wide. The largest of the arches is the southernmost and the smallest is the northernmost. All arches have rockpools, even at low tide, but walking through the largest arch can easily be achieved without getting wet feet. Walking through this arch brings you immediately to the eastern entrance to Smuggler's Cave 2.

Smuggler's Cave 2
13m
NZ 3659 7111

This cave is 4m high and is a simple walk through from the eastern entrance, to exit on the beach facing north, looking towards Brown's Point.

From Smuggler's Cave 2, turn left onto the sandy beach at Cullercoats Bay. In 1865 some fine specimens of fossil fish were found in the marl slate in this bay. The Permian bluff at the back of this haven contains four caves, which

The northern entrance to Smuggler's Cave 2

have been numbered from south to north and have collectively been known as Fairies' Cave for many years. The name may owe its origins to the Stuart period tobacco pipes that were found in the cliffs above. In the 19th century these pipes were known as fairy pipes because they were so small that the Victorians said that they had been used by fairies.

Fairies' Cave 1
13m
NZ 3641 7119

The first cave has a large triangular entrance and a sandy floor. It is walking height, with a slight bend to the right. At ground level in the cliff just north of Cave 1 there is a small triangular hole leading into a 4m flat-out crawl.

Fairies' Cave 2
17m
NZ 3639 7121

A big imposing entrance, with walking passages either side of a central rock wall. Both passages involve easy clambering over rocks and unite at the partly man-made rear wall. On the right-hand side of the rear wall is a final short crawl.

Fairies' Cave 3
19m
NZ 3638 7123

A sandy floored walking passage, on average 2m high and 2m wide.

Fairies' Cave 4
8m
NZ 3637 7125

This cave has a small, round entrance and a sandy floor. Crawl in on hands and knees for 6m, then the final 2m on the left is a flat-out crawl.

Make a day of it

The Dove Marine Laboratory is located at Cullercoats Bay. Although this is a Newcastle University building, it occasionally offers public lectures and open days.

Just a few hundred metres north of Cullercoats Bay is Brown's Point, an interesting rocky section of coastline. With its uninterrupted views of the sky to the north, this is apparently one of the best places in the North East for viewing Aurora Borealis under the right conditions. Further north is Whitley

Bay, home to a long and popular beach and the famous Spanish City.

To the south is Tynemouth Longsands, an impressive mile-long beach that can be followed to the very pleasant town of Tynemouth, home to a priory and castle owned by English Heritage. For more information and opening times, see: **http://www.english-heritage.org.uk/visit/places/tynemouth-priory-and-castle/**

Minor Caves

I have included in this book everything in Northumberland that I believe warrants recognition as a cave. This county of course has other cavities in the earth that some would perhaps consider worthy of inclusion, and no doubt some that I have included would have been disregarded by others. As a general rule, I have included all the known naturally occurring hollows in the rock with a length or depth of more than 5m. A few smaller caves have been included if they are in very close proximity to other, larger caves. Caves, or rock shelters, formed by large overhangs or spaces underneath boulders have only been given individual entries if they are particularly interesting, e.g. St Cuthbert's Cave.

Some minor caves, such as Rob Roy's Cave, Macartney's Cave and Little Church Cave, have been mentioned alongside other caves. There are several other cavelets in Northumberland that may be of interest to readers, including, in no particular order, the following:

- An old farmstead at Muckle Samuel's Crags in Wark Forest, NY 683 788, has been constructed from rock from the crag. There are two small caves underneath overhangs.
- On Ravenshill Moor, near Kielder, at NY 629 957, there is a tiny cave under an overhang: Peden's Cave. Alexander Peden was a leading 17th century Presbyterian from Ayrshire, who is said to have used this cave for the baptism of a local man, William Robson.
- Edwardian visitors to Gilsland Spa are said to have been treated to the soothing sounds of a piper in Piper's Cave, at NY 636 681. A good footpath from Gilsland Spa Hotel leads to the unusually-shaped Popping Stone, where Sir Walter Scott is said to have proposed to Charlotte Carpenter. Although the Popping Stone is in Cumbria, Piper's Cave is across the River Irthing and therefore in Northumberland. The 3m long, 14m wide overhang under a sandstone outcrop is usually barely visible through dense vegetation.
- There is a medieval shieling, or temporary home for a shepherd, known as Woolfe Kennel Cave, at Kennel Crags in Wark Forest, NY 639 784. This is formed from the space underneath a large boulder and features a porch and a roughly paved floor.

- There is another cave in Northumberland called St Cuthbert's, or Cuddy's, Cave. This is found at NU 004 310, on Gled Law south of Doddington. It has almost certainly been artificially enlarged for use as a shelter but at the back of the cave is a tiny elliptic tube, which appears to have formed in the same way as Roughting Linn Cave. Although a very small cave, with dimensions of 2m wide x 1.3m high x 1.3m long, it is worth a visit, as is the nearby hillside of Doddington Moor, which is blessed with cup and ring marked rocks, standing stones and hillforts.
- At Hepburn Crags, NU 074 247, near Chillingham, there are several small rock shelters within the very large boulders. These small caves seem to have formed by mass-movement in the Fell Sandstone, in a similar way to Cateran Rift and Cateran Hole.
- There is a spectacular sandstone arch at Cloudy Crags, west of Alnwick at NU 147 135.
- Too small to be a cave, barely even a cavelet, but the rock shelter at Kettley Crag, at NU 075 298 near Chatton, is worth visiting for the extraordinary cup and ring marks. Please do not enter this rock shelter as that would mean stepping on the prehistoric petroglyphs.
- Henhole Crags on the Cheviot, at NT 888 203, contain some very small caves. There is a local legend about Black Adam of Cheviot, who robbed and murdered a bride on her wedding night. Pursued by the groom, he leapt across the gulf of Hen Hole and hid in a cave, where the groom found him and they fought until 'their twa bodies went crashing doune the steep'.

Glossy of Caving Terms used in this Book

Aven – A shaft, not open to the surface, rising up from a passage.
Blind – A term used to describe a passage or chamber from which there is no way on.
Caving – Exploring caves of any kind.
Chamber – A room in a cave, generally with larger dimensions than the approaching passage.
Chockstone – A stone that is wedged in a vertical rift.
Choke – A blockage in a cave passage, usually by fallen rocks.
Chossy – Characterised by loose rock.
Duck – A section of cave that involves lowering one's head towards or into water.
Karst – Characteristic limestone landscape, shaped by water dissolving the rock.
Oxbow – A loop formed by the former path of the stream, but usually now dry.
Phreatic development – Cave passage development by water under pressure. Existing cracks are enlarged in this way, entirely underwater.
Potholing – A term usually reserved for exploration of caves that include vertical sections.
Resurgence – The point at which an underground stream resurfaces.
Shakehole – A hole or depression in the ground caused by water erosion, usually found in limestone. Surface water disappears down shakeholes and often forms caves beneath. Although most dictionaries treat this as two separate words, cavers generally treat it as just one. The same goes for streamway.
Sink – The point at which a stream goes underground.
Speleology – The scientific study of caves, although this term is often also used to describe the recreational activity of exploring caves.
Speleothem – Deposits, usually mineral, on the walls, ceiling or floor of a cave. From the Greek speleon, cave; and them, deposit.
Sump – A section of the cave that is completely underwater.
Thrutch – To climb into a space by an inelegant method.
Vadose development – Cave passage development by a streamway with an airspace above. The water is thus not under hydrostatic pressure and erosion is of the floor of the passage.

History of Caving Guidebooks that have included this region

Although this is the first guidebook to be written exclusively about the caves in Northumberland, there have been earlier caving guidebooks written for much larger areas that have included brief entries for some of the caves in this county. All of these books are currently out of print, but well worth acquiring should the opportunity arise.

Pennine Underground by Norman Thornber, with maps by Arthur Gemmel, was first published in 1947. A second edition in 1953 was retitled *Britain Underground* and was written by Norman Thornber, A.H. and R.D. Stride and J. O. Myers, with maps again by Arthur Gemmel. In 1959 there was a third edition, back to the name *Pennine Underground* and again written by Norman Thornber, with maps by Arthur Gemmel.

In the 1970s, the first *Northern Caves* guides were published, initially in five volumes. A handful of the caves in Northumberland were described in *Northern Caves Volume 5. The Northern Dales*, by D. Brook, G. M. Davies, M. H. Long and P. F. Ryder, which had its first edition in 1974 and second edition in 1977. The second series of *Northern Caves* guidebooks adjusted the geographical regions, so Northumberland's entries were now in *Northern Caves 1. Wharfedale and the North-East*, again by D. Brook, G. M. Davies, M. H. Long and P. F. Ryder, published in 1988. A third series is in production, with the first book, *Northern Caves. The Three Counties System and the North-West* by Sam Allshorn and Paul Swire, having been published in 2017.

Cave discoveries are usually recorded in the journal of the caving club that was involved in the initial exploration. Of particular note are the journals of the Moldywarps Speleological Group, which give detailed accounts of the exploration of many caves in the north of England. *Descent*, the magazine of underground exploration, is published bi-monthly and down the years has included a number of articles on caves in Northumberland.

In addition to these caving guidebooks, magazines and journals, below is a selected bibliography, listed chronologically:

Wallis, John. (1769). *The Natural History and Antiquities of Northumberland: And of so much of the County of Durham as lies between the Rivers Tyne and Tweed; commonly called, North Bishoprick*. London: W. and W. Strahan

Hodgson, John. (1820). *A History of Northumberland in Three Parts.* Newcastle upon Tyne: E. Walker

Mackenzie, Eneas. (1825). *An Historical, Topographical, and descriptive View of the County of Northumberland.* Newcastle upon Tyne: Mackenzie and Dent

Sopwith, Thomas. (1833). *An Account of the Mining Districts of Alston Moor, Weardale and Teesdale.* Alnick: W. Davison

Partington, Charles F. (1836). *The British Cyclopedia of Literature, History, Geography, Law and Politics.* London: Orr and Smith

Richardson, Moses Aaron. (1846). *The Local Historian's Table Book, of Remarkable Occurrences, Historical Facts, Traditions, Legendary and Descriptive Ballads &c., &c., Connected with the Counties of Newcastle-upon-Tyne, Northumberland and Durham. Volume 5.* Newcastle upon Tyne: M. A. Richardson

Strickland, Agnes. (1852). *Lives of the Queens of England: From the Norman Conquest.* London: Lea and Blanchard

Tomlinson, William Weaver. (1888). *Comprehensive Guide to the County of Northumberland.* London: Walter Scott Ltd

Tomlinson, William Weaver. (1893). *Historical Notes on Cullercoats, Whitley and Monkseaton.* London: Walter Scott Ltd

Lumley, D. (1934) *The Story of Tynemouth Priory and Castle.* Newcastle upon Tyne: Northumberland Press Ltd

Smith, Ian. (1988). *Northumbrian Coastline.* Warkworth: Sandhill Press

Earl, John. (2004) *Northumberland Climbing Guide.* Northumbrian Mountaineering Club

Waddington, Clive. (2004). *Maelmin – a Pocket Guide to Archaeological Walks.* CountryStore

Crowe, Steve and Earl, John. (2008). Northumberland Bouldering Guide. Northumbrian Mountaineering Club

Ryder, Peter. (2008). *Memoirs of a Moldywarp.* Broomlee Publications

Lowes, Andrew. (2016). *A Walker's Guide to the History of Northumberland.* Ammanford: Sigma Leisure

Index

Alloa Lea Quarry Cave	75
Ayleburn Caves 1 and 2	97
Ayleburn Mine Cave	90
Ayleburn Pot	94
Bellcrag Cave	78
Berwick-upon-Tweed Sea Caves	118
Cateran Hole	25
Cateran Rift	28
Coe Crag Cave	36
Crag Point Caves	140
Cullercoats Caves	144
Doubting Victoria Cave	31
Elpha Green Caves	110
Hartburn Grotto	72
Hartleycleugh Quarry Cave	100
High Cove	52
Huel Crag Rifts	46
Key Heugh Caves	56
Lindisfarne Caves	133
Nine Year Aud Hole	40
Pupienus Hole	38
Queen's Cave	81
Roughting Linn Cave	19
Rumbling Kern Caves	137
Seagull's Welly Pot and Resurgence	103
Shaftoe Hall	69
Simsholm Well	87
South Yardhope Caves	49
St Cuthbert's Cave	22
The Wanney Byer	65
Thomas Wedderburn's Hole	33
Tutu's Welly Pot	106
Ward's Hill Quarry Caves	59
Wire Hole	62

About the Author

Chris Scaife has always had a passion for wild places. He started caving with the University of Newcastle Caving Club in 2001, and upon graduation joined Black Rose Caving Club. Much of his leisure time has been spent caving – in Europe, Asia, South America and Australasia, but particularly in the north of England. He has descended many of the UK's most difficult caves and has been involved in the discovery of a number of new caves and passages in the UK and abroad, including discoveries in Cumbria, North Yorkshire, County Durham and Northumberland. He has contributed numerous articles to *Descent*, Britain's bestselling caving magazine. When not caving, Chris enjoys walking, cycling and looking for wildlife in Northumberland and further afield.

More books from Sigma Press

A Walker's Guide to the History of Northumberland
Andrew Lowes
From the wild uplands of the Cheviot Hills and North Pennines, to the fertile valleys of the Tyne and Tweed and on to the magnificent cliffs and sweeping beaches of the coastal fringe, Northumberland has almost everything. The history is very special too, with some of the most influential events in British history having happened here. Stone, Bronze and Iron Age people, Romans, Dark Age Warlords and Christians, Reivers and Industrialists have all left their mark. It's all there to be discovered if you know where to look.
£9.99

Northumberland Walks
You Take the High Road
with alternative routes to suit all abilities
Anne Leuchars & Debby Waldron
Together they have devised walks which bring equal pleasure to both types of walker. Each walk splits into harder sections for fitter people and easier tracks for slower walkers. In most cases you all set off together, then separate part way through and meet up again to complete the walk together. The walks also accommodate differences in approach to a day in the countryside. Some people like the satisfaction of several miles or a steep hill conquered, others prefer to stroll along, taking rests along the way to relish the views.
£8.99

Discover Northumberland
30 coastal and inland walks
Mark Lejk

30 circular walks covering the whole of Northumberland aimed at people of all walking abilities and preferences with lengths ranging from 4.5 km (2.8 miles) to 17.8 km (11.1 miles) and difficulty ranging from easy to strenuous. Many of the longer walks have shorter versions and altogether the different variations and combinations make for 48 routes. The walks range from the fabulous Northumberland coastline to the Cheviot Hills, Kielder Forest, the North Pennines, Hadrian's Wall and there are a significant number of walks in the area between the coast and the Cheviots.
£9.99

Discover Northumberland Volume 2
30 coastal and inland walks
Mark Lejk

The second volume of Discover Northumberland contains another 30 circular walks covering the whole of Northumberland. It is aimed at people of all walking abilities and preferences with lengths ranging from 1.6 km (1.0 miles) to 22.3 km (13.9 miles) and difficulty ranging from easy to strenuous. The walks range from the far north of the county to the southern border with County Durham visiting the fabulous Northumberland coastline and the wonderful countryside inland along the way. Some of the walks are Northumberland classics but many are new, being specially created by the author.
£9.99

River Tyne Trail: sources to sea
Peter Donaghy & Peter Laidler
The stone at the North Tyne, near the England-Scotland border, was erected in October 2013 specially to mark the beginning of the trail. From tiny springs to streams and then vibrant rivers, the two sources eventually converge to create the powerful River Tyne as it journeys to the sea. The nature of the undulating terrain makes for a challenging and rewarding experience as the trail passes through some of Britain's most beautiful and interesting scenery. This book is the brainchild of former businessman Brian Burnie, the founder of the Cancer Patient Care Charity 'Daft as a Brush'. Brian hopes that this walk will promote the work of the charity which provides individualised transport for patients requiring cancer treatment.
£12.99

Northumbria Walks with Children
Stephen Rickerby
Over 20 walks are included covering the North East from the Tees to the Tweed. There are questions (with answers!) and checklists to both challenge and interest the children, as well as practical information for parents. All walks are less than 5 miles long, exploring the great variety of scenery and heritage of Northumbria.
'This is a splendid collection that will excite and stimulate youngsters.'
– Sunderland Echo

£8.99

Northumberland Place Names
Anthony Poulton-Smith

Some of the definitions give a glimpse of life in the earlier days of the settlement, and for the author there is nothing more satisfying than finding a name which gives such a snapshot. The definitions are supported by anecdotal evidence, bring to life the individuals and events which have influenced the places and how these names have developed. This is not simply a dictionary but a history and will prove invaluable not only for those who live and work in the county but also visitors and tourists, historians and former inhabitants, indeed anyone with an interest in Northumberland and the city of Newcastle upon Tyne.
£8.99

County Durham Place Names
Anthony Poulton-Smith

Some of the definitions give a glimpse of life in the earlier days of the settlement, and for the author there is nothing more satisfying than finding a name which gives such a snapshot. The definitions are supported by anecdotal evidence, bring to life the individuals and events which have influenced the places and how these names have developed.

This is not simply a dictionary but a history and will prove invaluable not only for those who live and work in the county but also visitors and tourists, historians and former inhabitants, indeed anyone with an interest in County Durham.
£8.99

Walking the Cheviots
Classic Circular Routes
Edward Baker
An excellent introduction to this solitary, wild countryside. Everyone is catered for from weekend family walkers to the experienced hill walker. Each route contains details of the natural history, geology and archaeology of the area. For ease of reference, the book is in two sections, covering the northern and southern Cheviots – distinct areas with their own unique character. There are almost 50 walks – by far the most comprehensive collection published for the Cheviots.
£9.99

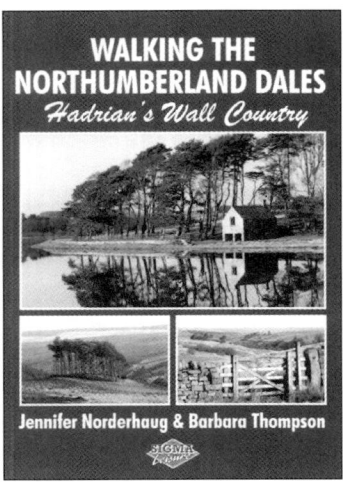

Walking The Northumberland Dales
Hadrian's Wall Country
Jennifer Norderhaug & Barbara Thompson
Discover and explore the lesser-known landscapes of the Northumberland Dales. The book includes routes in North and South Tynedale, Allendale, Hexhamshire, Blanchland and Hadrian's Wall, and routes within easy access of Newcastle-upon-Tyne, Durham and other popular locations – with forays into Cumbria and County Durham. It features 28 medium grade, cross-country walks.
£8.95

All of our books are available through booksellers and our website.
**Sigma Leisure, Stobart House, Pontyclerc
Penybanc Road, Ammanford SA18 3HP
Tel: 01269 593100 Fax: 01269 596116**

info@sigmapress.co.uk   www.sigmapress.co.uk